GUINÉ BISSAU 1984
Correios

1964-Innsbruck
1968-Grenoble

6p00
« SARAJEVO '84 »

$6

70m ski jump, Emil Zografski, Bulgaria

GRENADA
Grenadines

POSTE AERIENNE

RÉPUBLIQUE POPULAIRE DU CONGO

Saut à Skis

600F

ANNEE PREOLYMPIQUE CALGARY

Postes Lao
6k

CALGARY '88

NICARAGUA CORREOS
1990

ALBERTVILLE '92   C500

Winter Olympics - Albertville '92

GRENADINES of St.VINCENT 45c

90m Ski Jump Gold Medalist Matti Nykänen, Finland, 1988

TANZANIA 300/-

THE HISTORY OF
SKI
JUMPING

To John

from Tim

October 2005

THE HISTORY OF
SKI
JUMPING

TIM ASHBURNER

Quiller Press

Photo credits

The photographs on pages 2 and 69 are reproduced by permission of Christies. Some other photographs and drawings are reproduced from out of print books and details are given in the Bibliography. Every effort has been made by the author to contact copyright owners but in some instances this has not been possible.

First published in the UK in 2003 by Quiller Press, an imprint of Quiller Publishing Ltd.

British Library Cataloguing-in-Publication Data
A catalogue record for this book is available from the British Library

ISBN 1 904057 15 2

Printed in England by the Bath Press Ltd., Bath.

Quiller Press
an imprint of Quiller Publishing Ltd.
Wykey House, Wykey, Shrewsbury, SY4 1JA, England
Tel: 01939 261616 Fax: 01939 261606
E-mail: info @quillerbooks.com
Website: www.swanhillbooks.com

CONTENTS

Chapter IV Towards 2000

Chapter V The British at Home and Away

Chapter VI Technical

FOREWORD

This entertaining book is quite unlike any other work on skiing history, and I welcome its publication in the centenary year of the Ski Club of Great Britain. The Ski Club was founded on 6 May 1903 in the aftermath of all the excitement aroused by the first organised demonstrations of ski jumping in Switzerland at Glarus and Adelboden the previous winter. Like those in the Feldberg region of the Black Forest these shows awakened whole Alpine communities to the unlimited potential of skiing, and after a stumbling start the sport of skiing never looked back.

Tim Ashburner, a former downhill racer with national colours, takes us from the earliest developments of ski jumping to the present day. Quite apart from celebrating a hundred years of ski jumping in central Europe, the book's publication marks a time when the sport has finally succeeded in adjusting to the upheavals caused by the massive swing to the 'v-style' form of flight in the 1990s. The changes and adjustments made in response by the International Ski Federation are all updated and explained.

So many of our earliest skiers are brought to life again, as are those of the inter-war years when Alexander Keiller built a British ski jumping team that we were proud of. At last, within this, the first book on ski jumping history in any language, we have a lasting record of their deeds and even misdeeds!

Alan Blackshaw OBE VRD,
President, Ski Club of Great Britain

INTRODUCTION

The first inspiration for this book came with some exhilarating summer days many years ago. On 31 May and 1 June 1961, I had the unforgettable experience of being one of three Britons who took part in the great ski jumping show at Wembley Stadium. On 30 May, Sir Charles Taylor MP, who was Chairman of the sponsors Cow and Gate, held a reception at the Ski Club of Great Britain for all involved. Thirty-seven of the best ski jumpers from eight other countries in Europe and Scandinavia had flown in with team managers and distinguished veterans, and the air was blue with congratulations all round as hands pumped in welcome and the drink flowed. Many of the guests had been absorbed into the Third Reich during the War, and a visit to London for the purpose of ski jumping was something very special.

Sir Charles and the technical team were visibly relieved. In spite of a strike by scaffold workers, the huge structure at Wembley was in place, and stiff words to friends in the Government had ensured that containers of the very best (Class A) snow from Norway which was impounded by HM Customs where it was liable to melt, had been released, and was in cold storage in north London.

There were more problems next day when the elevator which was supposed to take the snow to the top of the slope failed to start at all, but like Iselin, in his moment of high triumph at Glarus fifty-eight years before, Sir Charles 'shone like the sun'. Whether he suspected it or not, his generous hospitality which continued backstage before and after our three performances contributed greatly to the fun. Some lads, particularly a few from regions far north, were plied with rather more than they were accustomed to, or even familiar with, and the number of spills on the hill reached the point where, in the final analysis, we three Brits finished in the unexpectedly lofty positions of thirty-fourth, thirty-fifth and thirty-sixth out of forty.

Importantly as far as these writings are concerned, I found myself for a few days in the company of such luminaries as the Austrian manager Sepp Bradl who before the War became the first man to jump 100 metres, and a host of others who feature prominently over much of the history of a sport that was only properly introduced to central Europe at the beginning of the century.

More than forty years on, the book marks the Centenary of the main phase of that introduction between 1900 and 1903, and also the Centenary of the Ski Club of Great Britain which was founded at the Café Royal in London on 6 May 1903. The early history of the SCGB is not unconnected to that of ski jumping. It was ski jumping that finally awakened the often apathetic Europeans to the enormous possibilities of skiing, and by introducing it to Davos in the winter of 1901/02, two of the Club's founders, Edward and William Richardson, aroused so much enthusiasm that in the summer of 1905 the locals set about building what was the largest jumping hill in the world. The pair travelled widely and contributed to the thrills and spills at Adelboden in 1903. The generous assessment of the Swiss pioneer Adolf Odermatt of their place in skiing history appears on page 43.

Some of our earliest pioneers deserve more than mere reference to their skiing exploits. It would for instance amount to a sorry omission if mention was made of Sir Arthur Conan Doyle without reference to the extraordinary place that Davos occupies in English literature, which seems all but forgotten.

The main emphasis of the book is on the early history of ski jumping up until the 1930s. After World War II the history becomes increasingly statistical as hills get larger, competitions proliferate at every level, and with the development of plastic surfaces it becomes a sport for summer as well as winter. It is the Olympics coming just once every four years which focuses attention more than anything else, and I have confined the records at the end to these alone.

In the late 1980s the process of evolution was swiftly accelerated as never before when the revolutionary 'V-style' form of flight was introduced. It was soon proved that once mastered, it carried the jumper much further than the traditional 'parallel skis' method. Hill sizes were increased considerably for top class competitions, but in order to maintain the sport's enviable safety record which is far superior to Alpine ski racing, certain adjustments and limitations had to be imposed.

Not all of the problems that came with the V-style have been solved but a hundred years after it first came to Europe, the future development of ski jumping appears easier to foresee. Women's' ski jumping on a K90 hill is likely to become an Olympic event, as is ski flying which may be included in the programme for Torino in 2006 for the giant hill at Planica in Slovenia is not far away. There are however only five ski flying hills, and environmental considerations may prevent the construction of too many of them, and perhaps shield the International Ski Federation (FIS) from the constant pressure from television channels for 'bigger and better' hills.

With ski jumpers routinely flying more than 200m on these hills, and with the women's record now at 170m, conservationists ask what is the point of further 'progress' when it is clear to everyone that the jumpers could glide in safety for much further if this was possible.

The book will serve a special purpose if it encourages someone somewhere to build the first modest plastic ski jumps in Britain, an objective which has defeated the British Ski and Snowboard Federation and its supporters over many years of confrontation with bureaucracy, vested interests, and 'the system' in general. Whoever achieves it will gain a lasting place in skiing history.

Britain is the land of the dry ski slopes. Up and down the country there are more than a hundred of them, but there is still not one ski jump anywhere. In Europe and Scandinavia by contrast, there are hundreds of plastic ski jumps, but no dry ski slopes at all. In countless towns and cities like Oslo, Willingen, Innsbruck, Fredstad and Predazzo, ski jumps of all sizes rise above the outskirts, beckoning to the adventurous spirit of local youth. Everywhere there are competitions for all age groups which attract sponsors, visitors and communal involvement.

Unusually such visible disparity with the rest of Europe seems to have escaped the attention of politicians hell bent on harmonisation within the EU. And yet this is an area where some level of integration would be worthwhile and popular. The British people are descended in part from the Vikings who invented the 'hopp' in their homeland more than a thousand years ago. Comparatively few of them ever see a ski jump, but no televised sport grips their imagination in quite the same way.

Certainly it makes compulsive viewing. A landing slope of dazzling whiteness curves from the crest to the length of the floor like the train of a Bavarian princess on her wedding day. Up and down the hill, the stands are packed to overflowing with stunning Nordic blondes, and giggling sun-tanned maidens from every land. And how they sing! The whole scene is several cultural shocks removed from the shabby terraces of British football, and when Eddie Edwards was 'called to the Bar' at the top of the tower in the 1988 Olympics at Calgary it was as if one of their own had reached the very pinnacle of the Gods, and that the ultimate white peril was about to be gloriously surmounted.

Inevitably such a giddy cocktail inspires a host of 'wannabes' many of whom we have tried to point in the right direction, while turning away those tiresome Ahabs who become obsessed with the idea that the Great White Ski Jump is something to be conquered, a short cut to fame and the adulation of those glamorous 'birds on the side' whose special contribution to the sport is not forgotten in these pages.

In Chapter I the reader will find Crichton Somerville's unflattering description of the lifestyle of young people in nineteenth century Oslo (as Christiania became known in 1905) before ski jumping was introduced in the years from 1879. It is a picture with which we are sadly familiar, but the transformation that he witnessed has been repeated many times elsewhere.

Now therefore is the time as we look ahead into the third Millennium for the government of Tony Blair and his bewildered Ministers for Sport, Education and Social renewal, and all concerned with urban youth, to look to the benefits and excitement that ski jumping brings to whole communities. Now more than ever before, as wars from the Falklands to Afghanistan have made clear, this country of ours needs tough young men, the types that are found on the rugger pitch, in the boxing ring and on the ski jumps. More and more, government policy over the years has shifted to the sell off of school playing fields and to the development of mollycoddles.

CHAPTER I
EARLY HISTORY
UP TO 1900

The beginnings of ski jumping

Getting from one farm to another in Norway in winter often involves a climb on skis up one side of a hill, and ski jumping developed as a means of clearing obstacles when skiing down the other side.

For centuries skiing was a means of getting about for peasants, hunters, and sometimes the military, with ski jumping cropping up in the sagas and early writings as a social activity and competitive sport in country areas.

Records of distances cleared in a single 'hopp' in primitive times are unclear, and somewhat left to the imagination like the story of Trysil Knut who jumped over twelve of the King's soldiers standing shoulder to shoulder. Trysil lived in the early years of the nineteenth century at the same time as Olav Rye who in 1809 jumped 9.5 metres on the slopes below Gamle Aker Church on the south-eastern outskirts of Christiania. Rye's is the first metric record, but in order to clear twelve soldiers, Trysil Knut must have flown a few metres further.

One of the very first competitions on record took place at Tromso, far beyond the Arctic Circle in 1843. Among the competitors was Johannes Wilhelm Steen who was sixteen at the time, and became Prime Minister from 1891 to 1893. He was born in Christiania in 1827.

Skier jumping off a wall into a courtyard

A vanished age of ski jumping in Britain

Many writers have left descriptions of Britain under heavy snow in times long past. One was Richard Blackmore who refers to the use of skis on Exmoor in his romantic novel *Lorna Doone* which was published in 1869.

In the February 1904 issue of *T.P's Weekly* there appeared a letter from a gentleman in Cumberland who signed himself as 'W.T.' describing the sport of skiing in the dales of Yorkshire and Durham in the middle of the nineteenth century. He himself had often gone to school on skis some forty years earlier in the 1860s.

W.T. wrote that it was not uncommon practice in those days for the Weardale miners to go to and from their work on 'skees', and that it was a fine sight to see thirty or forty men sliding down a steep slope from the mines after work at a speed equal to that of a railway train. Among the youth, ski jumping was a favourite pastime, and he believed the practice was a very old one from the fact that he knew boys of his own age who had come into possession of 'skees' which were once owned by their grandfathers.

Sadly we know no more about those Weardale ski jumpers. Their feats may not be commemorated at the Durham Miners' Gala, but one can still look up at the old mine entrances overlooking Weardale today, and the boulders large and small conveniently embedded along the hillside which provided for the 'hopp'. It is similar country to so much of Norway.

If the era of snowy winters had lasted until the years between 1900 and 1903 when ski jumping was first introduced to central Europe, and the British themselves were going out to join in the fun, those little villages between Ireshope Moor and Stanhope would have gained lasting recognition for the justifiable claim that 'we've been doing it all along'.

Morgedal and Sondre Norheim

Behold him on the highest peak
Adjusting skis and bindings
With cap in hand he stands erect
Then plunges boldly down

You saw him race from steep to steep
With snowdust in his wake
Now in the air, now on the ground
Headlong down the hill

He leapt aloft from off the roof
And floated o'er the barn
Far down the hill he landed then
And stopped at Bjaaland's farm.

Thus wrote the clergyman and poet, Aslak Bergland, of Sondre Norheim's daredevil descent of Kvaevenuten. Thanks to Bergland, and to Torjus Loupedalen, the author of an interesting book on life at Morgedal in the 1850s, the visitor to the district today can still look up and pick out the lines that Sondre used to take down this and other steep slopes such as Kastedalen to the frozen lake Moskei where he finished up. Sagging roofs of old barns testify to secondary use, or abuse, as ski jump platforms, and there are the smaller Ofte and Donstad hills where the village children, including the Hemmestveit brothers, used to swarm round Sondre who was such a joy and inspiration to them. Here he would teach them the slalom (without gates), ski jumping and skiing across country.

From Bjaaland's farm was to emerge the last of the great skiers of the Morgedal era, Olav Bjaaland, winner of the King's Cup at Holmenkollen in 1902, and a member of Roald Amundsen's party of five men who became the first to reach the South Pole in December 1911.

Loupedalen, describing the almost medieval conditions in a rough peasant community, in what became the cradle of skiing, wrote:

> The community houses some 500 people, who it has to feed and clothe, and provide leisure and work activities. It cannot manage to feed them all: many must go out begging, and many others leave, especially for the communities in Western Telemark, and those towards the South of the country. They take their crafts with them - making shoes, harness, weaver's shuttles, - or go into service. But the community can provide fun for them. There is dancing on the village green in the summer, skiing in the winter, and the fiddle and the dancing all year round. And here we have the key to it: the energy and the go of the people in the community had to find release, expression and form, and they find it in skiing.

Sondre Norheim

Of Sondre Norheim, Loupedalen tells us that he was 'as poor as a church mouse'. Shuttle making was supposed to be his occupation, but whole winters were given to skiing, and very often there was almost nothing for the family to eat.

Sondre and his brother Eivind also made skis, and experimented with different types of wood, into which they rubbed all sorts of 'waxes', such as old cooking fat and chimney soot. Bindings consisted of loops of birch roots twisted over the toes, and around the heels of boots which were themselves almost as primitive.

Bergland must be responsible for much of the myth that surrounds Sondre Norheim, for not even a Jean Claude Killy equipped in this manner, could have made such descents as the poet's imagination would have us believe. He was not the first to invent the Telemark turn, or what became known as the 'Christie', but by introducing the latter to Christiania, he was responsible for the adoption of the name 'Christie'.

In 1866 the first ski competition in Christiania that we know of was held on the slope at Iverslokken below the Gamle Aker Church. It was decided to continue with it, and in 1868 after invitations had gone out to country districts, fifty competitors came from as far as Nord Ostedalen and Telemark. Sondre and two of his friends spent three days skiing over mountainous country to get there. By contrast the competition itself was an undemanding slalom as a test of style, and a cross country race with tiny jumps on the downhill stretches. Sondre won comfortably, and his name at last became known outside Telemark.

Skiers at Morgedal

On 8 March 1868, a month after his triumph in the capital, there was a big competition on the Haugeli slopes at Kvitseide, consisting of three laps of a course which included seven jumps on the downhill sections. Today we would call it a steeplechase on skis. Sondre had tackled many more hazardous courses in his time, but he probably never jumped further than here at Haugeli. They measured his longest jump at 50 alen – an alen being 0.677 metre, which made it 34m.

Fridtjof Nansen came to credit Norheim with the same distance in *By Ski over Greenland*, but the newspapers of that time in Christiania, quoted it as only 30 alen, and even then with some reservations, stating that 'the account suffers from a considerable amount of exaggeration'. Most historians credit him with a longest jump of 27m which was to remain a record until 1891.

The Iverslokken competition, and another at Sandvika, were discontinued because of the general indifference of the townspeople. For them, skis were not the essential means of getting about in winter that they were for the peasants. The Christiania Ski Club was however formed by, among others, Thomas Fearnley, a Norwegian whose family had emigrated from England some seventy years earlier. They were a small group, but it was due to their efforts that some Telemark peasants were induced to visit the capital to give a demonstration of ski jumping on Huseby Hill, on the western outskirts of the city, in February 1879. They were rewarded with a crowd of some 10,000 people, and from this point, ski jumping never looked back.

By this time Sondre Norheim had retired from competition, and in 1884, at the age of fifty-nine, he and his wife Rannei joined the ever growing number of their people leaving for America in search of opportunities, and escape from poverty. Their second son Olav had gone there six years before, and had written home with glowing accounts of the future that awaited them over there. Their other five children accompanied them. Sondre died in 1897 at the age of seventy-two, and was buried in the cemetery of the Norwegian church at Denbigh, North Dakota.

In 1952 when the 6th Winter Olympic Games were held in Oslo, the Olympic flame was lit, not at Olympia, but in the birthplace of Sondre Norheim at Morgedal. From there, after a brief ceremony at the Norheim memorial where the flags of the thirty nations taking part in the Games were hoisted, the flame was carried to the stadium at Holmenkollen.

Eight years later, the flame was once again lit inside that humble dwelling and was conveyed across the Atlantic, and across America, to California where the 8th Olympic Games were staged in Squaw Valley. No other athlete has been associated with the Olympic flame.

The visitor to Morgedal today will also find the museum which commemorates Olav Bjaaland and the important part he played in the expedition to the South Pole. Responsible for maintaining skis and sledges, he also acted as Amundsen's route indicator. As the fastest skier in the party, he skied on ahead to check for signs of crevasses, and the best routes around ice ridges, and would signal to the other four coming behind with the sledges and dogs.

Like the museum at Kongsberg, it is one of a small number of provincial museums which record the skiing achievements of the locals.

Huseby Hill, Christiania, February 1879

It has always been the great good fortune of British skiing that the pioneers of the sport among our countrymen were famous writers. D.M.M. Crichton Somerville, Sir Arthur Conan Doyle, Edward Richardson and Sir Arnold Lunn not only included writing among their professions, but they were the right men in the right places at the right time.

Crichton Somerville, who was then living in Christiania, was among the huge crowd which gathered at Huseby Hill in February 1879 to watch what was the most significant ski jumping demonstration ever held. It was not just a demonstration, but the inaugural competition for the King's Cup. At last an ancient sport of remote peasant communities of the snowbound outback was brought by the successors of Sondre Norheim to the prominent notice of the townspeople. Within twenty-five years, ski jumping was to be introduced by these same people of Telemark to America, and by the men they taught, to the Alpine countries of central Europe.

The visitors from Telemark were joined on the hill by some brave, if unskilled locals who were determined to be part of the occasion, for the Huseby slope was one which only a few years previously had been described as highly dangerous and impossible to descend when the snow was fast and in good condition. Crichton Somerville wrote:

The leaping competition proved most highly interesting, though in some respects, quite comical. Every man, except the Telemarkins, carried a long stout staff, and on that, so they thought, their lives depended. Starting from the summit, riding their poles, as in former times, like witches on broom-sticks, checking their speed with frantic efforts, they slid downwards to the dreaded platform, or 'hopp' from which they were supposed to leap, but over which they but trickled, as it were, and, landing safely beneath, finally reached the bottom somehow, thankful for their safe escape from the dreaded slide.

But then came the Telemark boys, erect at starting, pliant, confident, without anything but a fir branch in their hands, swooping downwards with ever increasing impetus until with a bound they were in the air, and 76 feet (23m) of space was cleared ere, with a resounding smack, their skis touched the slippery slope beneath, and they shot onwards to the plain, where suddenly they turned, stopped in a smother of snow dust, and faced the hill they had just descended! That was a sight worth seeing, and one never to be forgotten, even if after years such performances have been, in a way, totally eclipsed.

Mikkel Hemmestveit

Jon Hauge became that day the first winner of the King's Cup. In 1883 the Hemmestveit brothers of Morgedal scored the first of their four triumphs. Torjus, born in 1860, won, with Mikkel who was two years younger, coming second. Of the impact that these two young boys and their country friends has on the whole way of life in the capital, Somerville continued:

The wonderful exhibition of the peasants' skill naturally excited the greatest interest, and acted on the townsfolk like a charm. Their leaping was regarded as one of the wonders of the world, and in subsequent years people flocked to Christiania from far and wide to witness it. Then came the turn of the tide, the eyes of the city youths became opened – the eyes of those who during the long winter days had, for want of better occupation, frequented billiard rooms or ill ventilated cafes, where the seeds of idleness and vice lay ready to strike root. By degrees such old haunts became forsaken, for the attractions of the newly found sport proved greater than those of the bottle.

In 1883 Torjus and Mikkel Hemmestveit ran the first ski school in the world at Christiania. People flocked to their classes and many were to become famous skiers in their turn. Mikkel received the King's Cup in 1885 and 1886, and Torjus once more in 1888. In 1888 Torjus also won the first 50km race to be arranged before he and Mikkel joined the exodus to America. There the two brothers along with other Norwegian immigrants took the lead and won competition after competition in many states. In 1891 at Red Wing, Minnesota, some 25 miles south of St Paul, Mikkel jumped 103 ft (31.5m). This was the first jump of 100ft or more.

Torjus died in Minnesota in 1930, while Mikkel who had gone back to Morgedal many years earlier, died in 1958 at the age of ninety-five.

1880 – 1900 Learning the hard way

Sven Sollid who won the first Holmenkollen in 1892. In 1897 he and Cato Aall both jumped 31.5m at Solbergakken to become joint holders of the world record

At that first Huseby show in 1879 there was a cross country race as well as the ski jumping. The two formed a single event, the winner receiving the newly inaugurated King's Cup. There was some modification in 1881 when the event was so arranged that it represented a test of all that might be demanded in the process of a ski tour. The course opened with a jump, followed immediately by a cross country sprint of about 3km over violently undulating terrain. The intention was to reward the complete skier who could jump, climb, run downhill, and ski well over level ground.

In 1883 the event was separated into a jumping competition and a cross country race, along modern lines, but the two remained as mere parts of a single event. For fifty more years it would not be permissible to compete in one, unless also competing in the other, and it was not until 1933 that competitors could, if they wished, compete only in either the jumping, or the cross country.

The annual Huseby event was moved to Ullbakken near Frognerseteren in 1890, and in 1892 to the new hill at Holmenkollen. Construction of the slightly larger Solbergbakken soon followed, but it was decided that the competition for the King's Cup at Holmenkollen should remain the annual showpiece for the sport.

The Solbergbakken, Christiania 1900

At Solbergbakken in 1897, Cato Aall jumped 31.5m and in doing so became the first of the townspeople to hold the world record. He was then twenty-one and years later he wrote of the trials and tribulations that beset enthusiastic but mostly impoverished young skiers of his generation:

Oslo old town was not an insignificant part of the capital. There were many large and beautiful houses there, with lovely gardens and sculptures of Adam and Eve. The inhabitants were mostly drawn to work at sea; pensioned-off old skippers, pilots, customs officers and the like. We also had the town's strongest man, the 'herring eater' who swallowed a whole herring and then pulled it up again with a piece of string attached to the tail, and a well known port official who looked like a windjammer in full sail when he walked around in dark blue uniform. There were also some industrial magnates, and some who stood high on the academic ladder, one of them a well known professor who had a beautiful house at the foot of Ekerberg hill. So all in all, when the horse-drawn sleighs with bearskin rugs came to the ski competitions they included many elegant people in top hats and winter coats, and ladies wrapped in fur. It was a marvellous sight and cannot be compared to today's Holmenkollen with all the different coloured stretch pants and costumes.

The old town was an ideal place for youth who loved sport and the outdoor life. Immediately outside the front door was the Ekerberg hill and the Kvaener hill, and no-one stopped us from skiing in the road. We were on friendly terms with the constables except for the one we called 'Pigseyes', but he was such a lousy runner that we boys were not afraid of him. We skied every day as long as conditions allowed, but although there was plenty of snow, there was little in the way of equipment.

Take our ski suit for a start. It was our school uniform that we used to decorate with various sizes of woollen scarves, the longer the better so that it crossed around the throat and at least twice around the tummy. In addition we had woollen socks, knee warmers, gloves and hats that pulled down over the ears. That was the Christiania boy of the 1880s. We did not exactly freeze in such an outfit, but it was not what you would call efficient. There were no girls on skis in those days, they made their appearance in the 1890s.

It was our feet that suffered most, and there were few who did not have open sores all through the winter. Every evening we worked hard to nurse our toes back to life. Cream, bandages and massage were the normal routine. No-one who has not experienced open blisters when skiing has any idea of the torture we endured. Fritz Huitfeldt, with his columbian iron bars was not one of humanity's well-doers. If only the feet sat tight we could have suffered the pain, but the soft footwear never fitted the bindings. Normally we wore thick socks with felt-like soles. Lapp shoes lined with soft sedge would have been better, but they cost a lot; 8 to 10 kroner. A bit better still were leather shoes, or elk shoes, but they were even more expensive, and for that reason used by very few. Then came the running shoe which was of thicker leather and stiff sole. How we envied those happy few who possessed them, for full control was only possible through a combination of stiff soles within iron bars.

The question of bindings was just as important, and there was hardly any material on this earth which was not tested; leather thicker and thicker, and in several layers, bamboo sewn into the leather, steel thread, umbrella spokes, wire rope stolen from the railways, and softwood which we turned ourselves. Some people had the shoes screwed onto the skis, but as they were also walking shoes, not many could afford that. When ski jumpers in the 1890s started to reach 25 to 30 metres the danger of skis falling off in mid-air increased, and happened often. That was when some wise soul thought of using long rubber straps which went up round the front of the ankle, then back to be fastened to one or two screws behind the heel. I was his first candidate, there was a feeling of safety, and from then on I used them all my years as a competitor.

Early bindings and bo

Skis were made of all sorts of wood; the simplest being of spruce, the better ones of pine, but neither were very fast. Better it was to make skis of deciduous wood, but they were very susceptible to the cold. Ash, especially green ash, but difficult to get hold of. Oak was used but was heavy and expensive. Of the lighter types; beech, elm and lime were used. They were slippery and therefore fast.

Many boys had skis made from barrel staves taken off large 8m barrels. These had the advantage of not being too long, and because they were bent in the middle it was easy to turn them. They were not exactly first class jumping skis, but they were good for small hills.

Early ski bindings

There were few ski makers in Christiania, and most skis arrived with the farmers in the market in early February with a top price of 5 kroner. Little by little the sports shops started selling their own skis, and the quality improved, but so did the price. Early on waxing was not a problem because we only knew of paraffin and candle wax. Tar burning became common, but it was best to impregnate the skis with equal quantities of linseed oil and paraffin in the summer and let them dry in the sun. I did this a lot and the skis became hard and solid.

As the length of the jumps improved the skis were found to be too light and many competitors tried to do something about it. I cut mine up in the middle and inserted an iron plate. I used these several years and think they are now in the ski museum. No real skier in those days used sticks, that was considered to be soft, for the girls and for the elderly, but some used a long pine pole with a small basket which was of no use in the snow. Later came the collapsible double ash pole without the basket. All this was quite reasonable equipment and in tune with the presentations demanded of a skier in those days.

Cato Aall was a member of the Norwegian team which competed in the first Nordic Games in Sweden in 1901. He wrote this account of his early experiences in 1942 while he and his countrymen were under German occupation.

Fridtjof Nansen 1861-1930

At a trade exhibition in Germany in 1881 there appeared a photograph of a young man performing a Telemark landing on the bottom part of a ski jump. The photograph had been taken in a studio, with snow-clad trees on the wall in the

background. It made a nice 'action photograph' which in those early days of photography was otherwise impossible.

The boy was Fridtjof Nansen who had greatly impressed as the best of the Christiania skiers at the third of the annual Huseby events earlier that year. He finished seventh out of forty-seven competitors, and beat ten of the fifteen entrants from Telemark. He had lost only to the very best of them. One journalist wrote:

> Of falls there were plenty, and not only minor prophets bit the dust … only twelve or thirteen out of forty-seven managed the big jump, and of those two were stick riders, but of the remainder, only a handful set off with full speed in the approach run without braking, including F. Nansen.

We can only guess as to whether the photograph inspired anyone who was to be involved in the early development of skiing in the Schwarzwald, but ten years later Nansen cropped up again as the greatest protagonist that the sport of skiing has ever had, as the author of *By Ski over Greenland*. This was first published in the Norwegian language in 1890, but English and German translations came out the following year.

The book was the story of the crossing from East to West of Greenland's unexplored central region, which Nansen and his four companions accomplished in forty-one days in 1888. Delayed by the south bound current and its endless ice floes from reaching their starting point until mid-August, they spent the winter at the Eskimo settlement of Godthab on the West coast, and were picked up late in April 1889.

Of special importance was that the book also contained a great deal of information on skiing, with many illustrations to show how it was done, and came out at a time when the early pioneers in Europe were struggling, and in need of encouragement. Suddenly these oft-derided missionaries found compelling evidence, that sooner rather than later, they would win recognition as men of vision.

Fridtjof Nansen was born on 10 October 1861, the son of Baldur Nansen, a lawyer of Christiania, and his wife who was originally Baroness Adelaide Wedel-Jarlsberg, a member of Norway's small aristocracy. For both parents it was their second marriage, previous spouses having died, and to the six children they already had between them were added Fridtjof and Alexander.

Fridtjof's mother was one of the very few women to ski at a time when it was not considered right for them to do so. Her nephew, the diplomat Frederick Wedel-Jarlsberg was one of the first two Norwegian skiers to appear in Vienna when he was posted to the Austro-Hungarian capital in 1892. It was a most timely appointment as far as the promotion of skiing was concerned, for he was ideally qualified to recommend his cousin Fridtjof's book to the right people at the right time. One result was that in 1896 the Emperor Franz Joseph I donated a trophy when international ski races were held for the first time in Europe at Murszuschlag.

Unknown to the Emperor or anyone else, Nansen himself had taken up residence that winter, without having offered any downpayment of rent for the privilege of doing so, on the archipelago that had became known as Franz Joseph Land. Cut off beyond the 80th latitude, he was imprisoned in the deep freeze of the long dark Arctic winter.

A union with another famous skiing family was formed when Adelaide's daughter Ida Bølling, a half sister of Fridtjof, married Axel Huitfeldt. He was a partner in Baldur Nansen's legal firm, and a brother of Fritz Huitfeldt, the designer of skis and bindings who supplied equipment for the Fram expedition. As Secretary of the Association for the Promotion of Skiing from 1886 to 1893, Huitfeldt was a key figure in the arrangements of the Huseby competition, and its transfer to Holmenkollen in 1892.

The Nansen family home, Lille Froen, lay at the edge of the great expanse of Nordmarka, and for young Fridtjof, when not at school, the year was devoted to the sports of the season. Summer was the time for fishing, and he was unusual in his enthusiasm for swimming in the sharp cold waters of the fjord, but the day was to come when he was forced to plunge into the ice bound seas of Franz Joseph Land to retrieve two kayaks which had broken loose from their moorings with everything that he and his companion depended on. Autumn was for hunting, and winter for skiing. At the age of ten or eleven he attempted his first ski jump on the Huseby Hill, only to come off the in-run and vault into the snowbank on the side. His parents then placed Huseby out of bounds to him.

In 1880 he entered the University of Christiania to study zoology, and in the summer of 1882 joined the crew of a sealing boat, the *Viking*, to the Jan Maycn and Spitzbergen seas, and the seas between Iceland and Greenland to observe animal life in high latitudes and collect specimens. This led to his appointment as curator of the Natural History Museum in Bergen.

The snow was very poor when he competed at Huseby for a second time in 1884. The race had to be cancelled, and only the ski jumping was held. This time Nansen finished ninth out of fifty-three competitors, but it was his week long journey overland from Bergen that became the stuff of legend. Partly by rail and boat, and even horse and sleigh, but mainly on foot or on skis over the mountains, he reached Christiania two nights before the competition.

In spite of many outstanding achievements as a long distance skier, Nansen's plans to cross Greenland on skis were greeted with disbelief. Even in Bergen the local newspaper waited until the expedition had departed before announcing: 'In June curator Nansen will give a skiing display with long jumps on the inland ice of

Fig. 63.

Fig. 66.

Drawings from By Ski over Greenland

Greenland. Reserved seats in the crevasses. Return tickets unnecessary.'

The thousands of air travellers who nowadays criss-cross Greenland every day on flights between Europe and North America would find such comments entirely justifiable. In summer when the clouds permit a view, Greenland presents an awesome sight, and as for the great carpet of ice floes that drift down the east coast, it is a wonder that Nansen's party reached their starting point at all.

They returned as heroes. Most people had come to assume that no trace of the party would ever be found again. For Nansen himself, came invitations to lecture in London, Bristol, Edinburgh, and on the continent, and numerous female admirers also. Then came his next job as Curator at the Museum of Comparative Anatomy at his old University, and it was through his research into the animal nervous system that he became one of the founders of neurology.

Realising that there was a current which might take a ship through the heart of the North Polar region, he conceived a plan to cross the Arctic Ocean in a specially constructed boat, the *Fram*, by drifting in the ice from East Siberia to east of Greenland. Setting off from Christiania on 24 June 1893, the *Fram* made a final call at Vardo on 20 July. With a crew of thirteen, and powered by steam and sail, it pressed along the Arctic coast and entered the ice north of the East Siberian Islands on 20 September. Eighteen months later, seeing that the *Fram* was going to by-pass the Pole, Nansen and Hjalmar Johansen left the ship at 84° 4" on 14 March 1895 with sledges, dogs, and kayaks for use on open water. On 8 April at 86° 14" they were forced to turn back by storms and the great ridges of broken ice that barred their way, and retreated south.

In August after covering seven hundred miles with great difficulty they reached Franz Joseph Land. Still north of 80° they spent the winter in a stone hut they built themselves, subsisting on a diet of polar bear meat and walrus blubber which also provided fuel for their lanterns and cooking. Temperatures reached as much as 76° below.

On 19 May 1896 they were able to leave the hut and continue south. It was thereabouts that they would have perished had Nansen failed to recover the drifting kayaks, an experience which he described as the worst of all. But on 17 June 'great things happened' as Johansen put it. Alerted by the distant barking of dogs, Nansen set off to investigate and met Frederick Jackson and his English expedition. Eight in number, they also had spent the winter on Franz Joseph Land, and it was in their cabins that 'we filthy black savages from the ice desert were given warm baths, soap, soft towels, clean clothing, proper chairs to sit on, a well spread table with civilised foods, and knives and forks to eat with'. Great was their triumph, but what of the *Fram*?

On 28 July the *Windward* arrived with fresh supplies and relief members of the expedition, and it was on this ship that Nansen and Johansen returned to Norway. They first called at Vardo which they had left more than three years before, to send numerous messages from the telegraph office. They then continued to Hammerfest where Nansen was astonished to find his friends Sir George and Lady Baden Powell on their splendid yacht, the *Otaria*.

On 20 August while they were enjoying further English hospitality on the *Otaria* a messenger came hurrying with a telegram which read:

Skjaervo, 20.8.96 9am

Doctor Nansen,
Fram arrived here today in good condition. All well on board. Leaving at once for Tromso. Welcome home.

Otto Sverdrup

Sverdrup had been one of Nansen's companions on the Greenland expedition, and it was with exultation that both the *Windrush* and the *Otaria* set off for Tromso. The *Fram* was sighted in the approaches to Tromso and it was on the high seas that the happiest and most exuberant of reunions took place. After Trondheim the *Fram* was left to make its way to a tumultuous welcome at Christiania.

In 1905 when Norway was struggling for independence from Sweden, Nansen played a decisive role in strengthening the spirit of the Norwegian people, and in mobilising world opinion. At one meeting a spokesman called to him: 'Take the helm Fridtjof Nansen! At this moment you are Norway's flag!'

After independence he became Norway's first ambassador to London from 1906 to 1908, and but for his refusal to join the state church, he could have become Prime Minister. He did a great deal with the League of Nations to help refugees and victims of Russian famine after World War I, and was awarded the Nobel Peace Prize in 1922.

Such was the towering personality who in his youth was one of the best ski jumpers of the day, and whose best-seller sounded a trumpet call for the sport of skiing.

Crown Prince Olav (later King Olav V) jumping at Holmenkollen in 1922

From Telemark to America

With the saga of the Norwegian emigration to the new world comes the introduction of skiing to America. In 1825 the *Restauration* set sail from Stavanger with fifty-seven emigrants, poor families filled with hope of a future. Over the next hundred years tens of thousands followed. They included most of the great ski pioneers; Sondre Norheim, Torjus and Mikkel Hemmestveit, Lars and Anders Haugen, and countless others, but the earliest had gone many years before.

The ski champions financed their trips by selling off their trophies which more often than not were made of silver from the mines at Kongsberg. The monetary value of these prizes used to be advertised by the organisers of the competitions at which they were awarded.

In the 1850s inhabitants of frontier mining communities in the Sierra and Rocky mountains used skis for many practical purposes, including the delivery of mail and supplies, hunting and railroad repairs. In some towns skis were so common that, according to one Californian newspaper: 'the ladies do nearly all their shopping and visits on them'.

The best known individual of those times was John 'Snowshoe' Thompson who was born Jon Torsteinsen Rui into a huge impoverished family in the Tinn district of Telemark. For twenty years from 1850 he skied back and forth, loaded with mail bags, over a mountainous 135km route between Placerville in California and Carson City in Nevada. In doing so he maintained communications across the range in winter when mail between the goldfields of California and Washington took four months.

Snowshoe Thompson was only forty-nine when he died in 1876, but in Illinois where other members of his family had settled, ski competitions began in 1863. With the coming of the elite of Telemark in the 1880s ski clubs grew up all over the Mid-West, notably at Ishpemming, Michigan, where the first formal ski jumping competition was held in 1887. No record of length exists, and the hill was probably very small, but the winner was Mikkel Hemmestveit who had arrived from Norway a few months before.

Torjus and Mikkel Hammestveit

Mikkel completely dominated the early American ski jumping competitions. To begin with he was based in Norman County, Wisconsin, whose ski club had been specifically founded so that when he won the one hundred dollar prize 'Ada and Norman County would get a share of the honour'. In 1888 he moved to St Croix Falls, Wisconsin, to set up the factory on behalf of the Hetting family and their Excelsior Ski Company. The larger of the growing towns where he performed were quick to see the commercial potential and prestige that ski jumping could bring. St Paul, the capital of Minnesota, sitting aside the Mississippi, had a population in 1890 of 130,000 and was well able to promote the new sport. Advertising over wide areas, backed up by hotel and restaurant promotion, excursion rates on the railroads and paddle steamers, and specially constructed grandstands, brought in thousands on competition days. To the fury of the people of St Croix Falls, St Paul claimed Mikkel Hemmestveit as its own after he won their first prize for the second time, as did the much smaller lumber town of Stillwater. As jumping became all important, a class of professional, or 'expert', was fostered, and cross country racing went into decline.

In Scandinavia cross country racing was designed to test a skier's all-round ability on all terrain, and ski jumps of various sizes were included along the course. In the Mid-West there were few natural hills where a competitor might start at the top, lift off a bump on the way down, and finish his run at the bottom. Jumps therefore had to be constructed artificially, and ski jumping could no longer be part of a race.

The question of prize money caused much soul searching among those who were anxious to preserve the true spirit of Idraet, the long held belief that the morality of the individual, as well as his physical and mental wellbeing were best developed through healthy exercise in God's great outdoors. Although money had sometimes been awarded to winners in Norwegian tournaments, the outright bid for cash never had the materialistic attraction that it did for immigrants in America. As tournament organisers offered extra inducements to 'good riders', and jobs to keep them in their towns and train the next generation, the prize money increased annually. By 1908 there were several clubs distributing $200 or more to top finishers. This represented a lot of money at a time when two or three dollars a day was the going wage for a miner in iron ore and copper belts of Michigan.

Mikkel Hemmestveit did not stay long in St Croix Falls, for he moved to Red Wing,

Minnesota, where he continued to be involved in ski manufacture. His brothers Torjus and Torgeir left Norway to join him, and the three went from town to town in Minnesota, Wisconsin, Michigan and Illinois. At Red Wing in 1891, Mikkel became the first man to reach the 100ft (30m) mark with a jump of 101ft. Two years later Torjus managed 103ft (31m) on the same hill.

At Ishpeming in 1905 the National Ski Association was formed under Carl Tellefsen to bring order to the sport, and take over the running of the National Championships that had been started at Ishpeming in 1904. There was a need for conformity in ski jump design, and a recognised method for awarding points for style. It was also in the interests of everyone that the lengths of 'record jumps' should be properly measured, and no longer entrusted to saloon bar keepers with lengths of rope notched with rags.

For the first three years from 1904 the Championships were held at Ishpeming. In an attempt to protect the ideals of Idraet the NSA decided to abolish all cash prizes. The result was that the jumpers decided to boycott the meet. Fearing that the tournament would not take place at all, the organisers were immediately forced to guarantee 'every wish of the riders' and put up an extra $200. They were particularly incensed and sad that some of their own Ishpeming boys were involved, but there was nothing they could do about it. However noble the intention of keeping the National Championships untainted, the money had to compare with what could be picked up elsewhere. Later a separate Amateur Day was set aside for non-professionals which had the advantage of spreading the jumping over two days.

Anders Haugen jumping above a car lot in Los Angeles in 1949 at the age of 58.

The winner of the 'National A Class' in 1904 was Conrad Thompson of Ishpeming. The location was moved to Ashland, Wisconsin, in 1907, and then in 1908 to Duluth, Minnesota, where the American record was taken to 117ft (35m).

Now and again the amateurs who were often schoolboys had their special moments of glory when they joined in on Professional Day. In 1911 at Chippewa Falls, Wisconsin, 10,000 spectators watched a German youth, Francis Kempe jump 118ft (36m) and 121ft (37m) to wrest the title from Anders Haugen who accomplished 117ft (35.6m) and 120ft (36.5m). Quite unexpectedly the biggest thrills came afterwards. The boys, for fear that they would cut up the slope, had to jump last, with the result that when their turn came the in-run was very fast indeed. Roused by the massive crowd, the fourteen year old Melvin Hendricksen went for it and cleared 131ft (40m). Then came Teddy Larsen, fifteen, who jumped 129ft (39m). In American slang, the boys 'slipped one over the professionals'.

A few weeks later Anders Haugen set an American record of 152ft (45.5m) at Ironwood, Michigan. He and his brother Lars won the National Championships eleven times between 1910 and 1926. Lars scored seven of these wins but it was Anders who represented the US at the first two Winter Olympics of 1924 and 1928. The story of how he came to be awarded his 1924 bronze medal at the age of eighty-three is recalled on page 62.

CHAPTER II
SKI JUMPING COMES TO CENTRAL EUROPE

The beginning of skiing in Europe

After all the excitement at Huseby in 1879, and the inauguration of the King's Cup, it was only a matter of time before skiing would be 'reintroduced' to central Europe, and on a much wider and lasting basis than had previously been seen in primitive eras. The industrial revolution had introduced an extensive railway network across the continent, and ten years after the Franco-Prussian War, people were enjoying a period of peace which lasted until 1914.

Skis, instruction and inspiration were all needed in equal measure, and all were to come one way or another from Norway. The British also played an important role which continued long afterwards with their development of downhill ski racing, for they tended to visit Norway much more often than the central Europeans, and as a result were the first foreigners to gain skiing experience there. Crichton Somerville who was a spectator at that first Huseby show was one of them, but a number of others were later to bring their Norwegian skis to different parts of the Alps, and to Switzerland in particular.

The first of such men was Cecil Slingsby who in 1880 made what was probably the first ski excursion of any sort in Europe by crossing the Kaiser Pass (1,550m) in the Kitzbuheler Alps above Kufstein. Two other Englishmen whose names are sadly unrecorded, made a ski ascent of the Brocken (1,902m) 80km south-east of Hanover. Colonel Charles Napier who went to live in Davos in 1888, arrived with a Norwegian manservant whose prowess as a skier caused a sensation.

In the Bernese Oberland, Mr Knocker brought with him three pairs of skis from Norway when he settled as a farmer at Meiringen in 1890, and Gerald Fox, another who had skied in Norway, introduced skiing to Grindelwald the following winter. Both had great success. In *Glarus 1905* there appears a vivid description of Gerald Fox in Grindelwald in a delightful tribute to his hero by Fritz Steuri, the first Swiss Champion in the Dauerlauf. We get the impression that the profession of skilehrer in the Oberland began with the chap who came behind Fox to fill in the holes. Was he sent by the Kurverein?

Later visitors to Norway included Charles Wingfield in 1892, the brothers Edward and William Richardson from 1895 onwards, and Sir Marcus Conway who used skis on his explorations of Spitzbegen in 1897.

In the very beginning the European pioneers somehow had to manage without the benefits that the British gained from their visits to Norway, and there were a number of abortive starts. Like Henri Duhamel of Grenoble, who noticed a pair of Swedish skis at the Paris Exhibition in 1878, they felt a sudden urge to try for themselves.

In the Schwarzwald, where farms are as widely scattered as in Norway, farm hands and forest workers were using skis in the 1880s. In doing so, they inspired others in the region including Dr Pilet in Colmar across the Rhine. Dr Pilet was one of three

Europeans who first put on Norwegian skis in the years around 1890, and who went on to play leading roles in the earliest development of skiing in Germany, Austria and Switzerland. The other two were Max Kleinoschegg of Graz, and Christoph Iselin of Glarus.

It was at the very moment when the efforts of these and other individuals scattered across the Alps needed a boost, when so often subjected to ridicule, that the German translation of Nansen's famous book was published. *By Ski over Greenland* made a great impression everywhere, not just because it was the account of a remarkable expedition which could only be achieved on skis, but because Chapter III, with its ten illustrations, provided instruction for cross country ski running, and for ski jumping. It was an enthusiastic commendation for a sport which was still virtually unknown to the world outside Scandinavia.

Nansen's book was even to motivate the man who came to be recognised as the 'Father of Alpine Skiing'. Mattias Zdarsky, a retired school teacher, lived at Lilienfeld, 60km west of Vienna. Deeply impressed by the book, he wrote off to Norway to obtain a pair of Telemark skis such as were used on the Greenland expedition, but found them difficult to perform with on steep alpine slopes. He had to find more practical methods.

When, in 1896, Zdarsky published his theories based on stem turns ('snow plough') and the use of a long pole to assist turning and braking ('stick riding'), there was enormous controversy. Some of his ideas were later rejected, but he furthered Alpine skiing in leaps and bounds. He had only one pupil at Lilienfeld in 1895, but over 1,200 came to his classes in 1905, and special trains brought devotees up from Vienna every Sunday.

Austria 1892/93

The snow came early in the winter of 1892/93 to herald the arrival of Norwegian expertise in Vienna, and the real beginnings of skiing in Austria. Frederick Wedel-Jarlsberg was installed at the Norwegian-Swedish consulate, and as a cousin of the newly famous Fridtjof Nansen, was in an unusual position to influence developments. An illustrated lecture which he gave to the Agricultural Society led at once to the formation of the Nieder Osterreicher Ski Verband on 8 November 1892. It was not quite the first ski club in Austria, for the Erster Vienna Ski Club had already expired. But now, more than one hundred pairs of skis were ordered from Norway, and the whole consignment arrived before the winter was over.

People in Vienna also saw ski jumping before 1892 was out. W.B. Samson, like Wedel-Jarlsberg, was also from Christiania, and was working in Vienna to complete his training as a master baker. Taking off from off a manure heap on a slope just out of the city, he jumped 8 to 10 metres, and everyone cheered. They had just seen the first ski jumps made in Austria, the distances being much the same as those made by Kjelsberg and Krefting at Winterthur in Switzerland two winters before.

These new initiatives, coming so soon after the publication of Nansen's book gave fresh encouragement to Max Kleinoschegg and his small band of enthusiasts in the Steiermark. In 1887, Max happened to see a picture of a skier in a British paper. He immediately wrote off to Norway, established contact with a skier, and through his

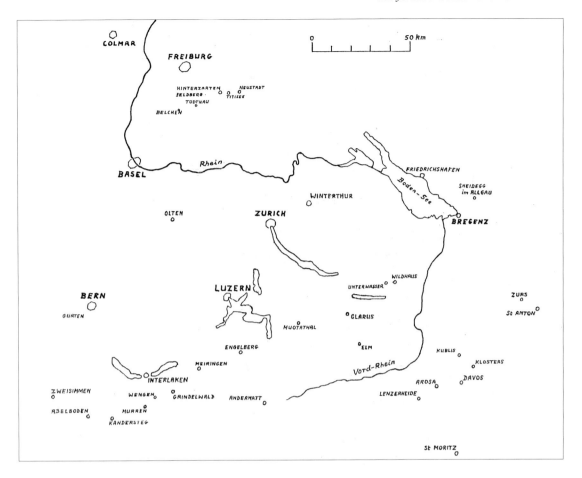

assistance obtained skis and a collection of pictures illustrating technique.

Over the next few years nothing special was achieved, but Max did find other devotees, and in 1893 they felt inspired to set up their Verband Steierischer Ski Laufer, and to set about organising some races at Murszuschlag, 80km south-west of Vienna. The first race was held on 3 February 1893, and did not attract many competitors but Samson was able to join them, and was an inevitable winner. The account which he gave later suggests that the real excitement came, not with the race, even though history recognises it was the first ski race held in central Europe, but with the ski jumping demonstration he gave afterwards:

> My skis were made by Eversen, a wheelwright from Slependen, and the spectators evidently thought that my speed on them was terrific. They asked me to jump as well, and I had a jumping hill made and flew like a bird through the air. At any rate that is what the spectators said when they told others about it later. They swung their hats, shouted and cried out, and then beamed when I landed down on the outrun after the jump. I waved back again. It was a great day.

There was no looking back, and Murszuschlag soon became the first Austrian ski capital. Ski jumping and downhill races were held in 1894, and the Alpenrose Trophy for cross country racing was inaugurated also, and won by Jonas Holmen who had been invited from Norway.

The Austrians continued to send invitations to the best Norwegian skiers for years to come. Karl Roll, who came with his brother Eyvind, won the Emperor Franz Joseph Cup in the first international ski race to be held in central Europe, in 1896. The field included three other Norwegians: Gustav Thaulow, Karl Sondresen and T. Monniche who were either studying or working in Austria at the time.

The Feldberg; the first European ski centre

In the 1890s developments similar to those at Murszuschlag had also begun 500km away in the Schwarzwald where country workers had started using skis, and where Dr Tholus in 1888 formed the Todtnau Ski Club, the first ski club in Europe.

Progress was held up by a succession of warm winters, but even so, the poor conditions were responsible for developments higher up on the Feldberg.

For many years people had come to visit the mountains for a few days in winter to escape the mud and slush on the plains. They were sufficient in number to make it worthwhile for Herr Mayer of the Feldbergerhof Hotel to keep his establishment open throughout the winter months instead of shutting up, as usually happened. The hotel lies at the height of over 1,200m and was the starting point for a popular toboggan run down to Titisee from where the railway runs to Freiburg.

Bjarne Nilssen at the Feldberg

Suddenly, on 8 February 1891, the enthusiastic Dr Pilet, the French Consul in Colmar, appeared at the Feldbergerhof with a pair of skis, and from that date the Feldberg effectively became the centre of a great deal of experiment and development such as had not occurred in Europe before. The Feldberg proved an admirable field to ensure rapid growth, and when we consider the close proximity of Freiburg, a University town full of energetic young men, we have the explanation why Dr Pilet, the first ski missionary in Europe, was so successful, and why the Feldberg became the first ski centre.

It was one of the University boys, Wilhelm Paulcke, who followed up the good work of Dr Pilet with a series of spectacular pioneering achievements which might even have included the introduction of skiing to Davos at the age of nine if the locals had taken any notice. Born on 8 April 1873, he was still only twenty when he was responsible for introducing skiing to a section of the German army for the first time, while on military service. In 1894 he went to the University of Freiburg, and in successive winters made the first ski traverse of the Feldberg, the first ski ascent of an Alpine peak over 3,000m (the Oberalpstock, north-east of Andermatt), and the first crossing of the Bernese Oberland glaciers. Each of these expeditions was carried out early in January.

In the meantime the Todtnau Ski Club joined with five other small clubs which had sprung up to form the Schwarzwald Ski Club in December 1895, and it was under the auspices of this umbrella organisation that the first races on the Feldberg were held in February 1896.

Feldberg

For some time it had been widely put about by Wedel-Jarlsberg and others who had been involved, that what the Europeans needed was top class instruction from Norwegian experts, either specially recruited, or living in the countries while working or studying.

In 1900 there was no one better qualified than Asbjorn ('Bjarne') Nilssen of Drammen, the Holmenkollen champion of 1897, and holder of the world record ski jump with a clearance of 32.5m on the Solbergbakken in 1899. He was twenty-four, and applied for a place at Freiburg University, and was duly enrolled in the autumn of 1899 as a student of medicine.

For the University and the Feldberg, Bjarne Nilssen represented a very big catch indeed. Welhelm Paulcke returned to the University a year later on being appointed Lecturer in Geology, but in Nilssen's first winter he helped the Schwarzwald Club to organise the first German Ski Championships of 1900. It consisted of a single, but strenuous event, a 30km Dauerlauf from Belchen to the Feldberg, and although 'open', it was decided to put Bjarne Nilssen into an 'International class' by himself, thus enabling a peasant named Maier to emerge as first national champion. Nilssen's time for the course was 3hr 9min.

Bjarne Nilssen

Nilssen pointed out that back in Norway all competitions included ski jumping, and after showing them how to build a small hill he proceeded to jump 15m. At Neustadt there was a site where they were able to build something more elaborate and he was able to fly 23m. His countrymen Kjelsberg, Krefting and Samson had earlier made the first small ski jumps in Switzerland and Austria, but these, the first seen in Germany, were very much longer, and onlookers were left thrilled. It was decided at once that ski jumping should be included as an additional event in the second German Championships in 1901.

Bjarne Nilssen decided that the spotlight should fall on the locals in 1901, and so did not compete. Without him there was no entry for the International race. Henry Hoek who now became champion was soon to meet with Edward Richardson, and they jointly wrote *Der Skilauf* which was published in 1905. It was not quite the first German language book on skiing because Wilhelm Paulcke had already written a book with the same title in 1890.

Lieutenant Bache of the Norwegian Army was studying at Charlottenburg University, Berlin, when he was persuaded to come in 1902. His jump of 29m made headlines everywhere. Christoph Iselin wanted him for Glarus in 1903, but found him unavailable. Thorleif Heyerdahl came to the Feldberg in 1903, having been feted like an emperor at Glarus just two weeks before, but after that the Norwegians refrained from competing until the Schwarzwald Ski Club celebrated its tenth Championships in 1910. Bjarne Nilssen was among those who returned for that special occasion.

The winners in the early years were:

Year	International Race	Ski Jumping		Schwarzwalder German Championships
1900	Bjarne Nilssen	Bjarne Nilssen	15m	Maier (peasant)
1901				Henry Hoek
1902	Lt Bache	Lt Bache	29m	Henry Hoek
1903	Thorleif Heyerdahl	Thorleif Heyerdahl	24m	= { Henry Hoek / Robert Biehler
1904	- Balke (soldier)	Karl Gruber	15m	Robert Biehler
1905	Karl Adolf	Karl Gruber	15m	Kaiser (peasant)
1906	Robert Biehler	- Walter	26m	W. Muller

Switzerland

In Switzerland the first 'skier' was probably Johann Imseng, a priest of Davos. In 1849 he was sitting in one of the inns when news came that one of his parishioners who lived 8km down the valley was dying. There was a need to hurry, and he ripped off a couple of staves from a barrel by the front door, and somehow fitted them to his boots. Off he went, as fast as he could, and he was apparently in time to deliver the last rites.

More than fifty years later Edward Richardson wrote that such was the shortage of skis in Davos that some of the local boys had to use barrel staves when they were persuaded to join in the fun during his first visit with his brother in the winter of 1901/02. Skiing had lost some of the momentum it had gained at Davos in the 1880s but there had been some remarkable pioneering achievements at Glarus, and in the Bernese Oberland where the British had introduced it.

The 1880s had seen the arrival of Norwegian visitors like the helpful chap who left his skis with the monks on the Grosser St Bernard pass enabling them to make copies, experiment, and even race one another. And there were those who came to work, like the school teacher and the butler at Davos, and Olaf Kjelsberg at Winterthur. They were few in number, but the impetus which they either provided, or actively encouraged,

Olaf Kjelsberg   *Christoph Iselin*   *Edouard Naef*

prepared the way for the students and others of their countrymen who were later to give the thrilling demonstrations of ski jumping which began at Glarus in 1903. Such was the impact of these exhibitions staged before large crowds that enthusiasm for skiing spread like a bush fire to every canton.

Of great significance was the partnership between Olaf Kjelsberg and Christoph Iselin of Glarus who met in 1891. Kjelsberg, born at Løddingen in Norway in 1857, came to Switzerland in 1881 and remained there until his death in 1924. An engineer by profession, he became director of Europe's largest locomotive factory at Winterthur, and often skied in his spare time, sometimes with another Norwegian engineer, Krefting. In 1891 he made a ski ascent of the Bachtel, a modest hill of 1,119m near Winterthur, and was soon contacted by Iselin who had made some unsatisfactory experiments with home made skis.

Through Kjelsberg, Iselin obtained from Norway three pairs of skis for himself, his brother Friedrich Iselin, and Jakob Jenny, for use in the winter of 1891/92. Kjelsberg and Krefting must be credited with the first ski jumps seen not just in Switzerland but also in Europe. On one occasion Iselin watched Krefting take off over a wall 2ft (0.6m) in height and jump no less than 8m before landing. When he reported on this astonishing flight to the Todi section of the Swiss Alpine Club he was greeted with mocking incredulity.

Undaunted, Iselin who at this time was a Lieutenant in the Swiss Army, realised that some recognisable achievement was called for, and enlisted Kjelsberg, Dr Edouard Naef who was also from Winterthur, and Alexander von Steiger for an expedition in the form of a crossing of the Pragel Pass (1,551m) from Glarus (472m) to Schwyz.

It is difficult today to appreciate the problems faced by many of the pioneers who were so often derided and ridiculed as men possessed with madness. Even cartoonists contrived to extract the utmost merriment from them with their unflattering portrayals, and it was in order to deny the sleeping citizens of even greater comedy that Iselin's party set off long before dawn on the morning of 28 January 1893. Had the people seen their departure they would have burst their sides with laughter, for not only were three of the party on the much maligned skis, but Dr Naef was using Canadian snow rackets, for the expedition was primarily designed to test the relative merits of skis and rackets in Alpine country. Dr Naef kept pace during the first day's climb to the chalet on the Klonthal where they spent the night, but once over the Pragel next morning he lost ground on the descent and reached Muotathal half an hour behind the others.

Very soon after his return to Glarus, Iselin made with Jakob Jenny a ski ascent of the Schild (2,302m) which rises above the town on 8 February. Dr Naef had climbed it in four-and-a-half hours on his snow rackets a month before, and the two skiers were to make their ascent in the same time. Their two hour descent however proved again that skis were the faster means of going downhill.

The Pragel and the Schild – and in less than two weeks! One represented the first genuine alpine ski expedition, and the other the first alpine summit climbed on ski. Ingrained prejudice suffered a notable defeat for suddenly Iselin and his friends found themselves the focus of much interest and admiration.

In 1799 the Pragel was one of the passes crossed by the army of the Russian Field Marshal Alexander Suvaroff in the greatest mountain march ever undertaken. It was now to take its place in skiing history. Newspapers paid tribute, and the wretched cartoonists were conspicuously outfaced.

Some important developments soon followed. Melchoior Jacober and his brother set up the first European ski factory in Glarus, Gebr: Jacober, and the Glarus Ski Club was formed on 18 November 1893. It remains Switzerland's oldest ski club.

Acting on Olaf Kjelsberg's advice, Jacober started to turn out two models. These were the Telemark ski with the same taper and specification as in Norway, and the Mountain ski, shorter (180-200cm) and wider (10-12cm).

In December of the same year, Hans Immer and two other men of Meiringen, where Mr Knocker had been active, made the first ski crossing of the Joch Pass (2,209m) between Meiringen and Engelberg. The route involves a formidable climb of 1,600m to the Pass, and this first crossing confirmed that the era of ski mountaineering had arrived.

Glarus at this time was a flourishing manufacturing town of some 5,000 souls, but down in the valley it had neither the snowfall, nor the length of season of the mountain resorts. Nor was there terrain comparable with the Feldberg to attract people to higher levels. It was not surprising therefore that it was another nine years before the Glarus Ski Club organised a race for the first time in January 1902. By this time however the ski clubs of Bern and Zurich had been formed, Norwegian students were arriving with skis, and the Richardson brothers were paying their first visit to Davos.

This first Glarus race was followed at once by another organised by the Bern Ski Club (founded in November 1900) on the Gurten which rises to the South of the city of Bern.

Grindelwald was meanwhile the only mountain resort where skiing had progressed. Dr Henry Lunn had been bringing British visitors there in winter for ten years, but in 1902 as Glarus entered its greatest era, he set his sights on opening for the new age of skiing an enormous number of resorts which were hitherto shut down.

At St Mortiz (1,740m) which had a better chance than anywhere else of becoming the first ski centre, the first impulse was smothered under the conservatism of the fashionable crowd. Less exotic was Davos (1,560m) the ancient capital of the Grisons situated at the end of the railway line which runs from Landquart via Klosters. The highest town in Europe, it had a combined population at Davos Dorf and Davos Platz of over 8,000.

At Davos Platz the British, at the height of their Empire, had yet another of their colonies, all of its subjects being there for reasons of health. Mr F. Faris-Barlow ran a boarding school for delicate boys (fees: £130 per annum) and Miss Dickens a similar institution for girls. Its residents and regular visitors included such men as Robert Louis

Stevenson, John Addington Symonds and Sir Arthur Conan Doyle who were not just great writers, but giants of the Victorian age.

In 1882 the local Swiss school had a Norwegian teacher, Agnes Duborgh on the staff. A young German boy, Wilhelm Paulcke, asked her to obtain for him a pair of skis from Norway. They were bought as a Christmas present by his father, a keen mountaineer who had often taken Wilhelm on small expeditions. From his first efforts with these skis Wilhelm Paulcke went on to became a great pioneer. After further schooling in Germany, and military service, he entered Freiburg University at a time when skiing on the Feldberg was fast becoming popular. In January 1897, with five companions, he made the first traverse of the Bernese Oberland glaciers from Meiringen to Brig. The route took them via Oberaarjoch, the Grunhornlucke and Bel Alp.

Another Norwegian, the nineteen year old Nils Nilsen, came to Davos in 1888 with a pair of skis, having been taken on as a manservant by Colonel Charles Napier who was living in Chalet am Stein above Hotel Buol. The chalet had previously been occupied from the winter of 1879/80 by Robert Louis Stevenson, and it was on the chalet floor that young Sam Osborne, the step-son to whom Stevenson was devoted, would unroll the curious looking map of *Treasure Island* as each sequence of the great story unfurled from Stevenson's mind.

> We did not think how far and wide through all the English speaking world the pirate romance would run, and what fame it would rapidly bring to its gifted author.
>
> In those days Davos Platz was a little workshop of brains and in the scuffle of proofs and projects some diamond dust went for lost. I have never lived in Davos a better time than I then lived. It was so full of beautiful Bohemianism, so sweetened by the strong clear spirit of the unique spirit whom all the world now claims for its own – R.L. Stevenson. So gracious and pure a light has never fallen across my path as fell from his fantastic and yet intensely human genius.

Thus wrote John Addington Symonds, the historian of the Renaissance, and founder of the Davos Tobogganing Club, who lived at *Im Hof* on the meadow.

'Villa am Stein' as the locals came to call it, also gained a reputation for theatre and puppetry, and now there was a further stir as the Norwegian butler came to and fro on skis, even making an elegant descent to the Buol with the Colonel's tea try balanced aloft on one hand.

Nils Nilsen later became a hotelier at Alesund in Norway. Local reaction to his skiing was not entirely negative. The guides Johannes and Tobias Branger made copies of his skis, as did a local carpenter, and in due course the Branger brothers became the first professional skiers in Switzerland. Teaching themselves, they had to go out at night to escape the uncomplimentary remarks of their fellow natives, just as Christoph Iselin was forced to do at Glarus.

On 23 March 1893, the Brangers accompanied by E. Burkhardt, made the first ski crossing from Davos to Arosa via the Mayenfelder Furka (2,445m). This came only eight weeks after Iselin's crossing of the Pragel, and when the Brangers repeated the crossing a year later they were accompanied by their client Sir Arthur Conan Doyle, the already famous creator of Sherlock Holmes. Conan Doyle first came to Davos in 1889 in search of a cure for his wife, having been offered the enormous sum of £1,000 by his serial publisher *Strand Magazine* for a further dozen articles. His own reading included Nasen's *By Ski over Greenland* which induced him to persuade the Brangers to send for several pairs of skis from Norway.

The skis arrived in the spring in time for some try-outs before the expedition to Arosa, a distance of 25km, and not without its perils. Conan Doyle described the hardest section as follows:

> You come to a hard ice slope at a angle of 75 degrees, and you zig-zag up it, digging the sides of your skis into it and feeling that if a mosquito settled upon you, you are gone.

Even when we allow for some exaggeration, this was still a remarkable performance for someone with very limited skiing experience using wooden skis with edges that offered little in the way of grip.

Eight years later the collection of skis which the Brangers now had in their possession proved to be of great significance. Edward and William Richardson arrived in Davos for the winter of 1901/02. In spite of their visits to Norway they were not equipped, but 'managed to unearth some skis from the shop of Mr Branger'. It seems as if they had gathered dust in the basement, but without these skis the Richardsons could never have started their very successful activities at Davos at what turned out to be a vital stage in the evolution of skiing in Switzerland.

E.C. Richardson

Edward Richardson was born in 1871. Unusually, he and his younger brother William are referred to by their first initials, E.C. and C.W, but together they played a major role in the introduction of skiing to Switzerland. With perfect timing they arrived on the scene at a time when the travel agencies of Henry Lunn and Thomas Cook were starting to bring winter visitors to the Alps from Britain, and just a year before Christoph Iselin brought the first Norwegian experts to Glarus.

The two were the sons of Mr D. Richardson of Hartfield Cove, Dunbarton, Scotland. By a curious coincidence, Mr A.J. Dowding, the headmaster of their first school, St Ninian's Moffat, also had two sons who distinguished themselves as skiers. The eldest, H.C.T. Dowding (later Lord Dowding) became President of the Ski Club of Great Britain in 1924, and gained more lasting fame as Air Chief Marshal in control during the Battle of Britain.

After St Ninian's, Edward went to Harrow, and then to Trinity Hall, Cambridge, from where he graduated with a law degree in 1892. In 1898 he became a barrister, but the new sport of skiing and his writings on the subject were already proving a more attractive occupation, and the law never took much part in his life at all.

The Richardsons first went to Christiania in the winter of 1894/95, but did not go together again until they both went to Davos in 1901/02. Their original intention was to go to Holland for some ice skating, but after being told that the possibilities for skating on the Dutch canals were grossly over-estimated, they decided to go to Norway where they found skiing instead, and ski jumping too. Jumping soon claimed both the brothers, particularly Edward who returned again in 1896 and in later winters. His own experience in starting to ski convinced him that jumping over small ramps was the best kind of practice for beginners. He was to prove this with great success at Davos a few years later.

In 1896 Edward became the first foreigner to jump on the Holmenkollen. He was

E.C Richardson

being taught at the time by Karl Roll, who as a twenty-three year old Lieutenant in the Norwegian Army, came second in the first Holmenkollen championships in 1892. Edward stayed on his feet in the process, but his distance went unrecorded as he was not taking part in the competition itself. Style anyway was more important than distance in those days, and when the 1896 Holmenkollen was held shortly afterwards in conditions of rain and slush, the winner Sigurd Svendsen put in two nice looking jumps on a day when forty-seven of the sixty competitors fell at least once if not twice.

In the same winter Karl Roll travelled to Murszuschlag in Austria where he won the Emperor Franz Joseph Cup in the first international ski races to be held in central Europe.

In later years the long service that Roll and Richardson gave to the promotion of skiing, and to the establishment of recognised competitions at every level, closely corresponded. The two Richardsons were among the small group which founded the Ski Club of Great Britain in May 1903. In the early years, as with the Davos English Ski Club, E.C, was the ruling spirit, serving in turn as Secretary, President and Editor of the Year Book. He became President for a second time when the Club celebrated its Golden Jubilee in 1953.

For his part Karl Roll was for many years Secretary, and then President of the Foreningen til Ski Idrettens Fremme (the Association for the Promotion of Skiing) which was founded in 1883, and under him the Norwegian Ski Association was set up in 1908. Realising the need for an international body, he organised the 1910 International Ski Conference in Oslo. This became the International Ski Federation (FIS) at Chamonix in 1924. He was a member of the Ski Club Ull (the Ski God) and his death at the age of ninety in 1959 coincided with the Club's seventy-fifth anniversary.

During his winters in Norway, Edward Richardson got to know all the best Norwegian ski runners, and made expeditions with them to the Jotunheim, Dovrefjell, Osterdalen and Finse. He also visited Sweden and in 1906 took an SCGB party to Are. From Switzerland they went to Stockholm where Richardson and Gideon Gibson took part in some local ski jumping, and then took the train for the long journey to Are on the line to Trondheim.

No less than ten business establishments in Christiania and Drammen took out advertising space in *Ski Runner* which Richardson wrote in collaboration with Crichton Somerville and W.R. Rickmers in 1904. They included respected gentlemen's outfitters and furriers, and long established suppliers to Arctic and Antarctic expeditions of 'toboggans, sleeping bags, mitts, lanterns, and all else necessary to ensure 'proper enjoyment of travel in cold places'.

It was the first book on skiing in the English language. A copy exists which is signed 'ECR. November 1903'. A second edition came out in 1905 containing an update on events at Glarus earlier that year, and a photograph of Leif Berg jumping 27m.

Also in 1905 Richardson teamed up with the famous Schwarzwald pioneer Henry Hoek to write *Der Skilauf.* Hoek won the German Championships in 1901 and 1902.

Davos 1901/02

Describing the state of skiing when they first arrived at Davos in the winter of 1901/02, E.C. wrote:

> We had come in search of snow, and found lots at Davos. The first thing that happened was that we were assured that Davos snow was, except quite late in the year, entirely unsuited to skiing. It was far too soft. Skiing could only be done on hard snow. A few people had tried it late in the year, but it was said skiing was not really at all suitable for Switzerland. This, however, we ventured to doubt, and we unearthed some skis from the shop of Mr Branger, and began experimenting. Naturally we soon found out the truth, namely that skiing was every bit as good at Davos as in Norway, if not indeed better. It was great fun, and we felt all the satisfaction of local explorers when we discovered the 'Church Slopes' and the long open run up behind the Fluela Hotel.

> When wending our way thither one day we were amazed to find some ski tracks other than our own. These proved to be those of Messrs Leeming and Fedden who we afterwards got to know.
>
> The boys of Davos came out to watch us practising on the Church Slopes. From this they derived great entertainment, but it was a long time before it seemed to occur to them that they might try a hand at the game themselves. This no doubt was partly due to the lack of skis. Eventually however some of them got skiing on barrel staves or something, and joined in the fun. We taught them the elements of running and jumping, and got up competitions, and so on.

Modest as they were, these were the first ski jumps seen in Davos and introduced a level of excitement that was previously missing. Events were to prove that in this their first winter in Davos, the Richardsons not only gave skiing a fresh start, but awakened the local people to the enormous sporting and commercial potential inherent in their mountains. It was also a most timely coincidence that their first winter at Davos was that which witnessed the first races in Switzerland organised by the ski clubs of Glarus and Bern.

Glarus 1902

Zurich, with its engineering and technical colleges, had long attracted more Norwegian students than anywhere else in central Europe. In 1878 these Zurich based Norwegians formed their own rowing club, and at some point in the 1890s some of them began to arrive with skis. In the 1896 issue of the *Norwegian Athletics Magazine* there appeared a letter from the rowing club with the comment: 'Of course when conditions are good, we forget neither skis nor skates. That we excel in the art of skiing, of course, stands to reason.'

At the turn of the new century the students included Finn T. Klingenberg who had competed at Holmenkollen, Kristofer Lund, Bernt Lund and G.A. Raabe. In March 1900, Kristofer Lund joined a party of Swiss in a crossing of the St Gotthard Pass (2091m) – on snow rackets! In spite of the achievements of Iselin, Immer, Paulcke and others, the Swiss still did not believe that skis could be used in Alpine terrain. When Lund returned in the following year however, he had with him a pair of skis, as did Finn Klingenberg.

Klingenberg was soon visited by Victor de Beauclair who had already achieved fame as one of Wilhelm Paulcke's companions on the first ski traverse of the Oberland glaciers from Meiringen to Brig. De Beauclair was full of enthusiasm for skiing, and the meeting resulted in the formation of the Zurich Ski Club on 13 December 1901, with himself as President, Klingenberg and Raabe as technical directors, and Kristofer Lund the Secretary. Club rules stipulated that a meeting would be held every Friday to prepare for the Sunday's skiing.

With the founding of the Bern Ski Club the year before, the Glarus Ski Club at last found itself joined by others and decided to hold its first ski championships consisting of a ski race, and hopefully some ski jumping.

Snow and weather conditions were awful on 27 January 1902 when the first ski race in Switzerland was held. A few soldiers who had skied all winter took part and the whole thing was rather unorganised with a geschmozzle start. The course was short and flat and competitors frequently had to stop to scrape their skis. The winner, to the surprise of many, was not one of the Norwegians, but Sub-Lieutenant Fritz Steuri from Grindelwald, who was also a postman. Owing to the storm it was not possible to hold the ski jumping, and Finn Klingenberg was denied the opportunity of giving the demonstration that had so eagerly been awaited. He gave himself no further opportunity to do so, for he left for America later that year.

Afterwards, Edward and William Richardson came over to Glarus from Davos, and Christoph Iselin now found that through the Norwegian lads and the two Englishmen he had contact with virtually the whole of the Norwegian ski fraternity wherever it was now spread. If some top class ski jumpers could be found, there was the prospect of being able to stage something quite dramatic. Twelve months later the dream came true.

Davos 1902/03

When the Richardsons returned to Davos for the winter of 1902/03 they were joined by a lot more English visitors including the brothers E.H. and J.B. Wroughton. On 6 January 1903 they got together to form the Davos English Ski Club. The main purpose of the club at this early stage was to pool subscriptions so that skis and bindings could be ordered from Norway for the general use of members.

It was going to take some time before the first shipment from Norway arrived, and although skis were being manufactured in Zurich as well as in Glarus, demand was fast outgrowing supply. The Swiss set up their own Davos Ski Club a few weeks after the DESC, and a large number of other clubs were to spring up after the great show at Glarus on 25 January.

Young disciples of Edwa and William Richardso show off their new foun skills

No sooner had the DESC been formed, when it had to deal with the large numbers who were anxious to join so that they could have access to the limited number of skis. The Richardsons were away in Adelboden, and so it was left to the Secretary, Colonel Swynfen J. Jarvis, to call a 'crowded General Meeting of seven members' on 31 January, at which he proposed a Third Class Test. They came up with the first ski test to be devised anywhere, and it consisted of four parts:

1. Stand still on the level for two minutes with no more than one fall.
2. Turn round without taking off a ski.
3. Ski down a moderate slope for 100 yards with no more than three interruptions.
4. Descend a steep slope erect once in six attempts.

Lest it be asked how such a 'Test' could possibly have exposed the 'frauds', it should be remembered that it was liable to be conducted in untracked powder, and with the use of flimsy equipment. In passing, the candidate could celebrate his admission to the elite.

Glarus 1903

A few days after the founding of the DESC the Richardsons were back in Glarus for the second great championships. Iselin had the exciting news that two Norwegian ski jumpers; Thorvald Heyerdahl, aged twenty-two, and Anders Holte, twenty-four, had been located up at Darmstadt in the German province of Starkenburg, and that after writing very long letters to each of them, found that they were both keen to accept his invitations to come to Glarus.

Heyerdahl and Holte had top flight skiing credentials, and had competed against Bjarne Nilssen back home. The success that their friend had enjoyed at the Feldberg encouraged them to follow, and they managed to enrol at an engineering college at Darmstadt. It was 230km from Freiburg, but the railway went there on its way to Basle.

In the mere forty-eight hours or so that they had in Glarus the two made skiing history, giving the first creditable demonstration of ski jumping in Switzerland. Anders Holte later told the story:

> We got there on 23 January in the evening. When I looked through the window next morning I had to put my head right out of the window to even see the sky above the mountains round the town.
>
> We were out in the morning to look at the hill which Iselin had appointed for the competition. But it was small and insignificant, and we had to jump right down to the flat to make 15 metres. We were therefore on the lookout for a better hill and found a suitable one where we could jump 25 metres. Iselin thought it too big, and there was not much snow. But I did not budge. After some discussion we got hold of some people who shovelled snow from the sides onto the out-run. The jump was built up with the help of branches on top.
>
> It was completed by the afternoon, and the sun that had been shining all day disappeared behind the mountain tops. So when Heyerdahl wanted to try the hill, it was frozen and rather dangerous. It did not go well, he fell and hurt himself. Iselin started to

Anders Holte

Thorwald Heyerdahl

become nervous, and insisted that the hill was too big, and that the organisers would not take responsibility if something happened. We calmed him down and said that we would take the responsibility. The hill was not nearly as big as Holmenkollen, and nowhere near the Solbergbakken where 36 metres has been jumped.

Next day, the day of the demonstration, the weather was wonderful, and the whole town turned up with many visitors – 6,000 the newspapers said. We were quite nervous ourselves when we waited at the top for the signal. This was something new in Switzerland and most people had never seen anything like it. Heyerdahl went first, and I heard the roar that immediately went silent, and I realised that he had fallen. Then there was another roar when the length, 18 metres, was announced.

Now it was my turn. The very moment I set off, all nervousness that had been there the last minutes was blown away. I let go, as always when I jumped, and all went well. I skied over the out run and stopped with a Christie. A chap ran over to me, hugged me, and shouted: 'You have saved the meeting!' It was Christoph Iselin. The length was given as 22 metres. It was as if the whole spectator mass started to gasp. There was adulation and wonder for me that was beyond any reason. For those spectators it had been a wonderful experience, a spectacle. Suddenly the band started playing 'Sons of Norway'. It was a solemn moment. Everybody stood listening with bare heads, and Iselin, who had of course got the band going, stood alone on the out run.

Later we jumped three more times, both of us without falling. And every time the crowd screamed their delight.

That evening there was a large feast in the hotel. Iselin shone like the sun when he distributed the prizes. My prize was a solid silver salver worth many hundreds of kroner. Immediately after the feast we students had to return to college. As we left the hotel the military band started up with a march. With the band leading, the members of the ski club carrying our skis, then us, the whole town followed. 'Make as though nothing,' Heyerdahl whispered to me, 'then they'll think we're used to this.'

It was not easy to pretend as though nothing was happening. No royalty could have been treated with more honour and admiration than us poor students who had only done a few lousy jumps on skis. When the train reached Zurich, G.A. Raabe who had attended the events, arranged a quick party, and the Norwegians were in high spirits.

A few lousy jumps? Edward Richardson who probably had far more experience of ski jumping than anyone else among the thousands at Glarus that day, wrote:

> The display of leaping and turning by Messrs Heyerdahl and Holte aroused great enthusiasm. Never had the people seen such a sight before, and the good seed sown took root and bore green shoots at once in the shape of numerous little jumps constructed by the juvenile population. And as in Glarus, so in other places, people were suddenly awakened by an exhibition of expert skill to the immense possibilities of the unwieldy looking boards.

The great leap forward represented an enormous triumph for Christoph Iselin, and placed the Glarus Ski Club on a pinnacle of its own. Pressed to return when their studies at Darmstadt permitted, Heyerdahl and Holte played important roles in bringing with them to Switzerland over the next two years some of the very best Norwegian skiers.

Neither Edward Richardson, nor his brother William, took part in this demonstration at Glarus, but afterwards they travelled to Adelboden where they participated in the first demonstration of ski jumping in Western Switzerland.

Adelboden 1903

Adelboden was meanwhile enjoying its first winter season through an agreement with the Henry Lunn Travel Agency. The Grand Hotel was open for the first time in winter and was often full.

According to his son Arnold, Henry Lunn never put on skis in his life, but fully aware of skiing's potential, he summoned Willy Rickmers, a disciple of Zdarsky who was married to a Scot, to come and teach his clients to ski. Lunn also inaugurated his Public Schools Winter Sports Challenge Cup. Because of class prejudices of the time it could hardly have been called anything else. It involved not only a ski race, but tobogganing and skating also. Some of his clients would have preferred snowball throwing to skating, but the trophy had a life span of eight years until 1911 when skiing and skating were given their own special trophies; the Roberts of Kandahar and the Lytton Challenge Cups.

The Bern Ski Club founded in 1900, had held its first races on the Gurten the previous winter, but now became more ambitious and advertised their first 'International Alpine Ski Races' to be held at Adelboden a week after the events at Glarus. They were also most anxious to emulate Glarus by staging a ski jumping demonstration, but who to get hold of? Heyerdahl and Holte were back in Darmstadt, and the only available candidates were the Arlberg pioneer Victor Sohm, the equally enthusiastic Dr Karl Gruber who divided his time between Munich and the Feldberg, and the Richardson brothers. Between them these four gave the first demonstration of ski jumping in western Switzerland.

Adolf Odermatt of Engelberg who later became a fine all round skier himself, recalled the action at Adelboden in a letter he wrote to Brigadier General Jack Wroughton in 1927:

> There is no doubt that the Richardsons introduced skiing into Switzerland. These two with

> Sohm and Gruber were the only ones who went over the jump at Adelboden in 1903. Gruber only, made three standing jumps of 16 metres. Sohm did 20m in a very fine style, and the Richardsons 14m to 16m, but they all fell, but anyway it was a marvellous and grand sight in those days.

Odermatt only narrowly failed to become Swiss champion on two occasions. A great friend of the British, he was an enthusiastic supporter of their development of downhill and slalom racing, and was the driving force in organising the first Swiss Championships in these disciplines at Engelberg in 1931. Like the Nordic events which were still open at this point, they were also made open to all-comers. The SCGB presented a Plate for the ladies' race which was won on that first occasion by Doreen Elliott.

St Moritz 1904

The great excitement aroused at Glarus in January 1903 even had the effect of awakening St Moritz to its enormous potential as a ski centre. Letters went off to Heyerdahl and Holte in Darmstadt urging them to come, and if unavailable to find other Norwegian experts to take their places. Inevitably there were other centres equally determined to get hold of them, but the result was that Heyerdahl arrived at Lenzerheide at Christmas 1903 accompanied by Trygve Smith. There they spent three weeks giving ski instruction to some seventy people before moving to St Moritz as guests of the newly established Ski Club Alpina which had scheduled its first competitions for 19 and 20 January 1904.

Trygve Smith and his younger brother Harald were both brilliant ski jumpers who were to feature prominently in Norwegian and European events for years to come. Trygve might have gone into the list of world record holders in 1899 when, aged nineteen, he reached what was the astonishing distance of 36m on the Solbergbakken. This was 3.5m more than Bjarne Nilssen had managed there in the same winter. That he was not generally credited with the record may have been because he started from a higher point on the in-run than he was supposed to have done, and put himself at risk by outjumping the hill. Instead it was Harald who became a world record holder when he jumped 45m at Davos in 1906, but Trygve went on to win the Holmenkollen in 1915 and 1917.

At Badrutt's Park the two Norwegians built a small ski jump on the site where the Julierschamze was inaugurated two years later, and in the first ski jumping competition to be held at St Moritz they led off with a demonstration double jump of 16.4m.. Six Swiss and two gallant British visitors then stepped forth for the Ski Club Alpina's first great championships. There were constant spills, and the winner Friedrich Iselin was the only one to stand on both his jumps of 12.2m and 12.4m. By staying upright for just one jump of 11.4m, H.P. Cox finished in second place ahead of Balthazar Caprez of Ponteresina whose best effort was only 'partly successful'.

The ladies' ski race which followed attracted three entrants, and in beating two local frauleins Miss Hamilton gained for herself not only the applause at the prize giving at the Kulm restaurant, but the first win anywhere by any British skier, male or female, in the history of skiing.

More was to follow, for when the Ski Club Alpina held their second meeting on 6

March 1904, the 6km Dauerlauf was won by Charles Wingfield. The course included 300m of uphill climb, but Wingfield who learnt to ski in Norway was an easy winner in just over fifty-four minutes. Carl Nater of St Moritz came second with a time that was five minutes slower. Eleven competed.

With his performance in the January event Cox became the first British ski jumper to gain a mention in the records of European ski jumping. It is very likely that Edward Richardson, who outjumped Fred Iselin at Glarus a year later, had already taken part in competitions in Norway, but no record remains. St Moritz was to become a base for much enthusiastic British ski jumping until the outbreak of World War II. In 1907 J.C. Young won the shield donated by the local doctor W. Biby. J.K. Greig, a British figure skating champion made his home there and introduced his nephew Alexander Keiller who amongst much else, founded the British Ski Jumping Club in 1926.

Glarus 1904

To the great disappointment of very many there were no Norwegian experts available to put on another ski jumping demonstration when the third Glarus Championships were held in January 1904. The Glarus Ski Club was the victim of its own success the previous winter. Other ski clubs were springing up, and Thorvald Heyerdahl and Trygve Smith had been enticed to Lenzerhaide, and then to St Moritz.

A jumping competition was held nevertheless and was won by Victor Sohm of Bregenz with 18.5m which was by far the longest distance achieved by a European to that date. No other details have survived, but in the cross country events, both the Richardsons and E.H. Wroughton did well for all three received invitations to visit other parts of Switzerland. One of these came from Joseph Voltz who had travelled over from Engelberg, but as in the previous year they decided to go to Adelboden.

Determined to regain the impetus which only ski jumping could provide, and to obtain proper ski instruction for their youth, the Glarus Ski Club decided they should invite young Norwegian experts to visit them for the winter of 1904/05. In August therefore, Christoph Iselin wrote to Anders Holte who was on holiday in Andalen, to invite two Norwegian boys between the age of fifteen and seventeen to spend the winter in Glarus. They had to be excellent skiers, especially in the Telemark and Christiania techniques, and good jumpers, 'and we want them to instruct the young of Glarus to ski properly'. The lads would be offered second class return travel, full board with the best families in Glarus, and free places in the excellent school where they could learn German, French and English.

Holte was horrified to think that boys of fifteen might be idolised and escorted in triumphal processions such as he and Heyerdahl had experienced, and tactfully replied with the suggestion that slightly older lads would be more suitable. He then approached the topmost echelon of the older juniors, and in Leif Berg and Thorleif Bjornstad he found two who were keen to accept the invitations.

Both were born in 1885. Berg was firmly established as the best junior ski jumper in Norway, having won the eighteen to nineteen year-old category at Holmenkollen in 1903 and 1904. Bjornstad finished third in the same category in 1903, and between them these two were to set the whole of the Swiss skiing fraternity, young and old, on fire.

Before 1904 was out Christoph Iselin managed to summon sixteen of the Swiss ski clubs together for the meeting at the 'Aarhof' in Olten on 20 November which resulted in the formation of the Swiss Ski Association. Albert Weber of the Bern club was elected President, and it was decided that when Glarus held the fourth of the championships in January 1905, they were to be accorded the title of the first Swiss Championships.

Discovery of the Parsenn Run, 1904

After staying awhile in Adelboden, Edward Richardson returned to Davos, and Joseph Voltz wrote again in the hope that he and the other Englishmen might find time to visit Engelberg. The visit was put off until 1905, but it is worth reading the letter that Richardson wrote to Voltz describing the discovery of the Parsenn.

Johann Engi

> Hotel Belvedere
> Davos Platz
>
> 5th March 1904
>
> Dear Herr Voltz,
>   Many thanks for your kind letter. I fear however that Engelberg is rather too far for me, and Wroughton is returning to England this morning.
>   Thanks to Dr O.Schuster we have discovered a new tour line which for a single day affair it will <u>I think be hard to beat</u>. It is as follows:
>   Start from Wolfgang (near Davos) and climb (mostly along a good path) <u>800</u> metres to the Parsenn Furka. Thence down to Kublis <u>1600</u> metres, distance 10 kilometres in a straight line! Thence back by rail to Davos. No risk of avalanches. Slopes nowhere too steep and facing North so nearly always good snow. Grand views of Alps and some delightful woodland scenery. <u>In fact by far the best tour I have ever made</u>.
>
> Yours truly
>
> E.C. Richardson

Dr Schuster who became famous for his explorations in the Caucasus was familiar with the route in summer, as was Johann Engi who was for many years chief guide of the Davos English Ski Club. It was these two who suggested the winter excursion to their English friends. In years to come it proved to be the most popular and best known ski run in the Alps.

On 13 January 1924, Fred Edlin of the SCGB inaugurated the Parsenn Derby which was first won that day by Peter Gruber of Davos. As a young boy Peter was taught to ski by the Richardson brothers, and he was in the party of young hopefuls who Edward Richardson took to the second Swiss Championships at Zweisimmen in 1906.

The Parsennbahn which eliminated the uphill climb was built in 1933, and was the giant of its time.

Glarus 1905

From the start when Glarus staged the first of the Swiss Ski Championships in 1905, a distinction was made between amateurs and professionals, with the guides competing in a separate category from everyone else. These were the few bergfuhrers or mountain guides from the Bernese Oberland who were beginning to find jobs in winter as Henry Lunn brought large numbers of British to villages that had hitherto hibernated. They were starting to gain some ability as skiers, but as ski jumpers could not do more than flop over the edge.

The actual Championships events were otherwise open to all nationalities, except for the Norwegian visitors who Iselin had imported to provide the demonstrations and the thrills.

Leif Berg's famous jump of 27m which was the longest seen in Switzerland to that date

The profession of skilehrer at this time was in its very earliest stage of gestation, but the idea was to segregate those whose work was assumed to equip them better for the grim ordeals of those early dauerlaufs when it was thought fit to include an enormous amount of uphill climb. However such a ruling had its shortcomings, and at once created the first 'shamateur'.

Fritz Steuri, a young Grindelwald postman, was accustomed to skiing a long and strenuous route every day in winter, and on foot in summer, on a round which took him up much of the Mannlichen side of the valley, and was paid to do so by the Post Office. With such rigorous training behind him, he was an easy winner of the 20km Dauerlauf run over the Pragel. The course included 565m of ascent and 1,162m of descent, and he finished in 1hr 54min.

The winner of the Jumping Championships was Victor Sohm who cleared 17m. Karl Gruber from Munich was second, and Edward Richardson third with 14m. Later Richardson wrote:

> I expected to find everybody very expert there, but was rather surprised to hear that they were expecting the same sort of thing of me. Luckily the three Norwegians turned up

and saved the situation, but I was here let in for trying a really big jump for the first time in my life. It was a very terrifying experience, but I acquitted myself fairly well and won third prize, with Herr Sohm first.

For their part, Berg with 27m, and Bjornstad with 25m, were well able to 'save the situation' to the noisy acclaim of another large crowd. The *Allgemeine Korrespondenzblatt* reported:

> The Norwegians Berg, Bjornstad and Holte shone with their long jumps and wonderful posture. Singly and in pairs they flew through the air like birds, daring and beautiful, soft landing like arrows down the outrun, and on the flat an elegant turn. And they stood still. No hard breathing indicated any nervousness or agitation. All was executed with perfect quietness and manly dominance.

Leif Berg

Thorleif Bjornstad

Richardson lost only to Karl Gruber who became German champion a little later with a 15m jump at the Feldberg, and Victor Sohm, the 'Father of Arlberg skiing' who founded the Arlberg Ski Club in 1901. On 1 January 1900, Sohm and two friends celebrated the arrival of the new century by making the first ski ascent of the Scesalphana (2,969m), and at Bregenz he and his partner Madlener manufactured or imported new bindings, wax, detachable seal skins, and climbing irons to fit aside the bindings.

Hannes Schneider who founded the Arlberg Kandahar with Arnold Lunn in 1927 was among his pupils when Sohm gave the first ski course in the Arlberg at Zurs in 1906. Then aged fifteen, Schneider was to follow his teacher by winning the Swiss Ski Jumping Championships three times while it was still open.

Fritz Steuri, the first Swiss champion in the Dauerlauf later wrote of his hero, the Englishman Gerald Fox who so much inspired him when he introduced skiing to Grindelwald in the winter of 1891/02:

That was an event! He had a room at the Baren Hotel. His skis belonged to him absolutely. Before he went out skiing, he trudged along the hotel passages in them, and when he came back in the evening the staff watched him from behind doors and curtains looking at each other and shaking their heads when he disappeared into his room, and with his skis on, for they were all perfectly sure that the tall Englishman must be mad.

He didn't seem a bit mad to me. I was thrilled with him. When morning school was over I often watched outside our chalet until he came down the street and practised on a slope close by. One day three people came out of the hotel. My skier had found a companion. With him was a guide. He was not wearing skis. No, he was carrying a shovel. What for? Just to fill up the holes in the snow!

I longed to try for myself all the things one could do with those bits of wood on one's feet. In 1898 my wish came true. I bought a pair of skis made by a Grindelwald carpenter.

Later I became a postman in Grindelwald. As the youngest employee I was given the most scattered and most difficult district, that around the Kleine Scheidegg and the Mannlichen. I had to cover 20km every day. In winter of course, my skis were an enormous help to me.

Among his countrymen Fritz Steuri became invincible, and although he was transferred to the Guides' category at Zweisimmen in 1906, he was still regarded as Swiss champion in the Dauerlauf. After winning for a third time at Davos in 1907, he readily agreed to the request of the race committee that he should retire to give others a chance.

The overall winner of those first Swiss Championships decided on the Dauerlauf and the Jumping was Friedrich Iselin, the brother of Christoph.

The Swiss Championships never returned to their original home again. Glarus could not compete with the new mountain centres which it did so much to awaken to their potential, and its famous pioneering role came to a close. Many years later however, Christoph Iselin's wish that 'the children of Glarus be taught to ski properly' was spectacularly fulfilled when there appeared another 'sweet daughter of Eve' who went forth to conquer the world, and to dominate women's skiing for eight years.

In 1988 when the last of the children taught to ski by Leif Berg were still around, the church bells of the little canton rang out in joyful triumph. Vreni Schneider, the shoemaker's daughter from the tiny village of Elm at the upper end of the Sernftal, won both the Slalom and Giant Slalom at the Winter Olympics at Calgary. She had already won the Giant Slalom at the World Championships the year before, and did so again in 1989. She was the winner of the World Cup in four of the five years between 1989 and 1993, and in the one year she did not win (1991) she won the Slalom at the World Championships instead. A career of unparalleled success culminated with another Olympic gold medal in the Slalom at Lillehammer in 1994, a bronze in the Giant Slalom, and a silver in the Alpine Combined. Vreni was twenty-nine when she retired as the most successful female skier who ever lived.

The Norwegians on tour

It was inevitable, given their personalities as well as their enthusiasm and expertise, that the visit to Glarus of Leif Berg and Thorleif Bjornstad should have been an outstanding success for all concerned. Arriving in mid-December, they conducted

Triple jump by Victor Sohm, Leif Berg and
Karl Gruber at Kitzbuhel, Austria in 1905

daily ski courses for as many as two hundred adults and children who were even taking time off school to attend.

In the December number of the *Norwegian Sports Magazine* for 1905, Berg described his first day in the job:

> I am off to inspect. A sweet daughter of Eve completely covered in snow, asks me to help her, and to tell her how not to fall. This was a difficult question and I thought about it for some time, and in the end said that the only way was to keep standing. She laughed and promised she would try. After lunch I sat down quietly and thought: It is an unusual thing I am doing here, but very nice.

After their demonstrations at the first Swiss Championships, the delighted Iselin was content to let them go off to the many other Swiss centres whose people were clamouring to have them. Over the rest of the winter they managed to visit seven of them: Les Avants, Grindelwald, Engelberg, Andermatt, St Gallen, Lenzerheide and Zuoz. The report of the course at Zuoz stated: 'Out on the hill everyone was ready and equipped with skis and sticks, young and old, rich and poor, students and professors, and also strict women.' Kitzbuhel was another destination.

At Andermatt they gave instructions to eighty officers and men of the Swiss Army, but a tour de force by Berg at Engelberg was to place him for all time in a class of his own. Setting off from the village (1,000m) he climbed to the summit of the Titlis (3,239m) from where he skied down to Trubsee in twenty-nine minutes. The involved a descent of 1,449m at about ·83m per second.

Today ski racers ride to the summits of the Titlis and countless other peaks in the comfort of cable cars, unconcerned with such inconveniences as a climb of almost 2,500m up a mountainside of powder and crust. With the additional advantages of ever updated equipment and carefully groomed pistes they achieve rates of descent that are ten times faster, and yet it was Berg who surmounted by far the more formidable test of true skiing.

Meanwhile Anders Holte had gone to Davos where he chose the site for a new jumping hill, the Bolganschanze, and advised on its design. At St Moritz, Trygve Smith did the same thing for the Julierschanze, and work on both was carried out in the summer of 1905.

Trygve Smith

When Trygve Smith returned to St Moritz for the winter of 1905/06 he brought his younger brother Harald with him, and the two gave courses up and down the Engadine. The locals, not merely content with these two, managed to entice Thorvald Heyerdahl once again, and even Bjarne Nilssen as well. Nilssen, who had long become the favourite adopted son of the Schwarzwald, had finished his studies at Freiburg and was able to come to St Moritz for five weeks. There was no shortage of class therefore when the Julierschanze was inaugurated on 23 January 1906. For the first time in Switzerland jumps of 100ft (31m) were recorded as they jumped singly and in pairs to the delight of all. Afterwards the clergyman Homann who was President of the organising committee warmly thanked them, and stated that these 'sons of Norway' should be thanked for introducing the new era of skiing.

Shortly before this, Thorleif Bjornstad had given demonstrations at Zweisimmen during the second Swiss Ski Championships which were held from 13 to 15 January. Afterwards he met up again with Berg and Holte for their visit to Germany. All three had invitations to Bayrisch Zell as guests of Karl Gruber and the Munich University Ski Club, and afterwards to the Feldberg for the Schwarzwald Ski Championships at the beginning of February. At the frontier they suffered the indignity of having their skis confiscated by the German Customs, and so were forced to use borrowed skis throughout their stay.

Such a fate did not befall the Smith brothers, probably because they had Bjarne Nilssen, who was returning to Germany, with them. To the great frustration of their hosts however, and the whole of the German ski fraternity, the keenly awaited showdown between the six outstanding Norwegians on the new jumping hill had been turned into an unequal contest before it even started. Trygve Smith's longest jump of 36m provided some measure of consolation, and was the longest jump seen in Europe to that point, but only for another month.

Returning to Switzerland, the Smiths' next destination was Davos for another much vaunted inauguration, this time for the largest ski jump in the world, the Bolganschanze, on 28 February 1906. Harald Smith set a world record with 45m. Trygve managed 46m, but a ski split on landing and he had a spill.

No one in Switzerland had yet jumped half these distances, but as Davos basked in its new found status as a major ski jumping centre, a great deal of credit for all that had so quickly come about was due to the Englishmen, Edward and William Richardson. It was only four years since they had first come to Davos and found skiing to be almost non-existent, and it was they who kick-started the sport by introducing the local boys to ski jumping, and thereby bringing some special excitement that was previously missing. In just three winters based at Davos they created the huge base of enthusiasm on which the Bolganschanze was built.

It was hardly surprising that by the end of that eventful winter of 1905/06 that Harald Smith and Thorleif Bjornstad should have decided to make their homes in Switzerland. There were to be many more action-packed winters to keep them fully employed. Smith who was now twenty-six, settled in St Moritz, while Bjornstad, just twenty-one, established a sports shop in Bern where he remained until his death in 1930. He became a respected figure and represented Switzerland at the International Ski Conference in Oslo in 1910.

The problems presented by the German Customs had been addressed when Leif Berg returned to the Feldberg in 1907, and he was marginally able to exceed Trygve Smith's earlier mark with 36·5m. In 1909 Harald Smith stretched his world record at Davos to 48m, and at St Moritz where the British had joined in the ski jumping with determination, he opened a ski factory in 1910. His two brothers Trygve and Hjalmar come to St Moritz for the Swiss Championships in 1911 and all three led off the ski jumping with a triple jump.

Zweisimmen 1906

The second Swiss Championships at Zweisimmen were spread over three days from 13 to 15 January 1906 to accommodate a range of events for the Juniors under eighteen, and under fifteen, and races for soldiers in the Swiss Army, and their patrols. Edward Richardson came over from Davos with a party of young hopefuls who included Anne Gibson and her younger brother Gideon, and also a local boy, Peter Gruber. All were to distinguish themselves.

Gideon Gibson finished a splendid fourth in the Junior Dauerlauf in 1hr 56min. This was only five minutes behind the winner, but ten minutes ahead of Eduard Capitti from St Moritz. Capitti easily won both the Senior and Junior ski jumping, and emerged as Swiss Champion. He was to win the title again in 1907 and 1911.

In the Seniors event, Capitti jumped 19·5m. The defending champion Friedrich Iselin, who came ninth in the Dauerlauf, managed 17·5m, and Richardson finished sixth, once again with 14m. There were ten contestants, and a few more in the Guides' Jumping where distances were all well short of Richardson's. When it came to the Juniors, young Capitti pulled out all the stops and cleared 21m.

A competition for boys under fifteen was held on a small jump giving distances of about 9m, and was won by Peter Attenhofer, with Peter Gruber second. Anne Gibson gained third place in the Ladies' Race, behind Fraulein Wyss and Frau Fischer.

Among the spectators at Zweisimmen were Vivian Caulfield and his wife who had just been introduced to skiing while on honeymoon at Chateau d'Oeux. Caulfield had an analytical mind and was particularly impressed that Thorleif Bjornstad, in the course of his demonstrations performed his downhill turns without the preliminary body movement that others employed to induce the turn.

It was the counter rotation technique that he was witnessing, and in his well illustrated book *How to Ski* which was published in 1910, Caulfield explained the mechanisms very clearly. The book had immediate and widespread influence, and the Zdarsky methods gradually disappeared from Alpine skiing.

Zeppelins take off too...

The first attempts by the Europeans to take to the air on skis in the first decade of the twentieth century coincided with man's first successful attempts to achieve the same thing in powered aircraft. Remarkably, some of the most dramatic developments of the latter sort were taking place at Friedrichshaven on the Wurtemberg side of the Boden See (Lake Constance). From there, in July 1900, Graf Ferdinand von Zeppelin's first airship, the LZ1, lifted off.

Two years later one of its successors made its celebrated flight to Luzern and back, and they became a regular feature in the skies over the very regions of Germany, Switzerland and Austria where ski jumping was beginning.

Man's ancient dreams of emulating the birds was being fulfilled in more ways than one, but primitive ski jumpers who gazed in awe, could only envy the effortless slow motion of these huge dirigibles, which were apparently able to float for ever. History was nevertheless to show, that with due allowance for lack of engine power, progress in the human form of flight, as represented by the ski jumper, was to keep pace all the way with advances in the mechanical forms. Furthermore the safety record of the ski jumper proved very much the better.

It would be flippant to suggest that the Zeppelins had any great influence in motivating the shovelling as ski jump construction got under way in earnest. Rivalry between the different centres competing for the special prestige which larger jumps were assumed to confer, was a major factor. Trygve Smith was able to jump 36m at the Feldberg in 1905, and in 1906 his brother Harald Smith set a new world record of 45m at Davos. And it was only four years since the Richardsons first came to Davos and found skiing almost non-existent.

On 17 December 1903, Wilbur and Orville Wright flew their first bi-plane at Kitty Hawk, North Carolina. Their airborne contemporaries, those early hoppers at Glarus, belong to the same venerated class, but as the likes of Harald Smith took ski jumping to a new level, so did Louis Bleriot with his first wobbly flight across the English Channel on 25 July 1909.

Chippewa falls, Wisconsin

Oscan Gunderson jumping 138ft at Chippewa Falls, Wisconsin, USA, 1911

CHAPTER III
BETWEEN THE WARS

The first man to achieve distinction in both forms of flight was the Scotsman, Alexander Keiller. In 1914 he became the first of his countrymen to jump 30m, and then became a seaplane pilot in the Royal Naval Air Service during World War I.

Keiller was not the only British jumper with pretensions to the Bleriot class before the War, but at the top level the first 60m jump was achieved by Henry Hall at Steamboat Springs, Colorado, in 1918, and came shortly before Alcock and Brown made the first transatlantic flight in 1919.

Charles Lindbergh's first solo crossing of the Atlantic in 1927 gripped the imagination of people everywhere, and a heightened awareness of the greater possibilities of flight was reflected in the level of interest in the ski jumping at the 2nd Winter Olympic Games at St Moritz in 1928. It was the most important ski jumping competition to be held anywhere to that date, and is recalled, together with the great controversy that blew up on page 65.

In 1936 the Austrian, Joseph (Sepp) Bradl, became the first to reach the magic 100m mark on the new 'monster jump' at Planica, Yugoslavia. The following year however, the graceful era of the Zeppelin ended disastrously with the explosion of the Hindenberg in New Jersey.

The Planica hill underwent further enlargement when the Nazis took over Yugoslavia, and in 1941 two Germans and an Austrian were able to take turns to set new records up to 112m. None would have stood any chance against Norwegians in properly organised competition, but as a spectacular propaganda stunt, it merely highlighted the difference between the capabilities of German ski jumpers and German aircraft. It was only three months since the Luftwaffe's disastrous Battle of Britain campaign had been called off.

By the time Concorde came into service in 1971, the ski jumper was cruising 165m, and neither Heathrow, nor even the Sea of Tranquillity ever witnessed a safer and more elegant touch-down. It was another twenty years however before the ski jumper decided to emulate the 'V-style' of Concorde, but by doing it the 'wrong way around' he was able to fly to the 200m mark and beyond. However, that is getting ahead of the story.

Alexander Keiller

At the 1908 Olympic Games in London figure skating events were included for the first time and held at the Prince's Ice Rink. Madge Syers was a clear winner of the women's event for Britain, while in the men's event John Keiller Greig came fourth. Greig, who was British Champion, was kept out of the medals by three Swedes, the winner being Ulrich Salchow, the originator of the jump which still bears his name.

Soon after the Olympics, Greig bought a winter home in St Moritz where he sometimes performed, and invited his nephews Adam Brown and Alexander Keiller to join him. In no time at all, all three got caught up in the excitement of ski jumping, and Edouard Capitti, the local boy who was Swiss Champion, was delighted to coach them. In 1910 they graduated to the Julierschanze and started coaching classes among the British, and set up competitions which attracted as many as ten. Greig brought to the jumping hill all the balance and co-ordination he had gained on the ice, and at a time when 30m on the Julier was phenomenal, and only reached by the Norwegians, he was a certain 25m man. In 1912 he did serious damage to his knee while performing some caricature on the ice, and an exhilarating sporting career which had brought entertainment to many, came to an abrupt end. For Alex Keiller however, these were the beginnings of a life-long involvement with the sport.

A Scotsman of Ballater, Aberdeenshire, whose family are still well known for their Keiller Dundee Marmalade, he was one of the most versatile of men. He gained fame as an archaeologist for his excavations and restoration of the megalithic stone circle at Avebury in Wiltshire where visitors can see the great collections of items unearthed in the Alexander Keiller Museum managed by the National Trust. He was an authority on witchcraft, criminology, and a great linguist. After Oxford, an eventful career as an aviator in the Royal Navy Air Service in World War I took him as far as Russia and the Middle East. Returning from one of his adventures by means best known to himself, he even turned up in St Moritz for a few days before returning to his unit.

After the War, Keiller became the leading light for a new generation of ski jumpers and langlaufers with St Moritz as their base. When the International Ski Federation was formed during the 1st Winter Olympics at Chamonix in 1924, he and Arnold Lunn became Britain's first two representatives. Although in his heart, his sympathies lay with the Norwegian traditionalists, he supported Lunn's efforts to gain FIS recognition for Downhill and Slalom racing. The two were sitting next to each other at the 3rd FIS Congress during the 2nd Winter Olympic Games at St Moritz in 1928 when the FIS voted to give these new disciplines a trial. As a result, the British were entrusted with organising the first FIS World Championships in Downhill and Slalom at Murren in 1931.

By then Keiller had founded both the British Ski Jumping Club and the British Langlauf Club in 1926, and was editor of their entertaining journals. On top of all this he also served as Secretary of the SCGB from 1920 to 1927, and until the Club acquired its first home in Palmer Street, Victoria, committee meetings were held at his London home, 4 Charles Street, Mayfair, where the shield of the Alpina Club St Moritz hung over the entrance.

In 1909 the Club inaugurated its first trophy, the SCGB Challenge Cup, to be awarded to whoever made the longest ski jump of the year. For the first three years this was achieved by Gideon Gibson who first came to prominence as a junior at the Swiss Championships in 1906. From Ayton in Berwickshire, he was one of that band of Scots who could hold their own with the Europeans in the early days. He went with Richardson's party to Stockholm later in 1906, and was credited with a jump of 25m at St Anton. By comparison, Hauptmann von Eccher who ranked as the best Austrian with Victor Sohm jumped 30m, and the new German champion, Walter, a student at Freiburg, 29m on the same hill.

"THE JUDGES'
ALEX. KEILLER
'HEGMATT' SPENCE

*Spence on left
and Keiller*

John Greig should have been awarded the Cup for at least one of Gibson's years, but did not bother with his application. Keiller won in 1913, but after becoming the first Briton to jump 30m on the Bolganschanze in 1914, he kindly ensured that the name of his friend C.C. Rolf went on the Cup that year. Rolf later fell in World War I, by which time mere modesty was not the only bar to finding the real winners. The rules stipulated that the lengths of jumps had to be verified by two qualified judges, but very often such luminaries were unavailable. Some felt that Kingsmill Delap's jump of 77ft (23·5m) at Murren was the longest of 1911, but the attestation did not fulfil the regulations.

After the War, the Challenge Cup was put in suspension with the following names and distances engraved on it:

1909	G.J. Gibson	70ft 6in
1910	G.J. Gibson	72ft
1911	G.J. Gibson	72ft
1912	E.C. Richardson	73ft 10in
1913	A. Keiller	85ft 4in
1914	C.C. Rolf	80ft 4½in

It is the only ski jumping trophy in the world to include a measurement to the nearest half inch, a tribute to the amazing accuracy of those dedicated specialists, the British ski jumping judges, but more likely a conversion from the metric estimates of two or more of them.

At Gstaad in 1911, the SCGB held the first British Ski Championships. These consisted of Langlauf and Ski Jumping, and did not provide much excitement. There were only five for the Jumping. Greig, Keiller, Delap and Gibson were among absentees, and great hopes of a magnificent contest fully matching anything to be seen in the Alpine countries at the time never materialised. The prospects of long train journeys to Gstaad did much to discourage attendance, as also did a deep reluctance to leave circles of friends in Murren and St Moritz, and adoring female fan clubs aside their jumping hills. The influence of the 'birds on the side' was to play havoc with even the best laid plans of organising committees for years to come.

It was left to Edward Richardson, then almost forty, to win the Jumping with distances of 57ft (17·4m) and 69ft (21m). N.S. Hind came second with 49ft (15m) and 58ft (17·7m), and there was special mention for Miss Hockin who 'very gallantly' went over the edge to record 25ft (7·6m) and keep her feet in the process.

A far more significant British initiative in that same year was the first downhill race for the Roberts of Kandahar Challenge Cup down a long demanding course above Montana sur Sierre in the Valais. Occasional downhill races had been held before but none had the influence that this did on the development of alpine ski racing after the War.

The British lost no time in building on their new creation when at last the peace came. A new generation at Oxford and Cambridge held their first ski race from Scheidegg to Wengen in January 1920, and this was followed in 1921 by the first British Championships to be decided on a downhill race. It was eight years before Austria became the first Alpine country to adopt the idea for themselves in 1929. The Swiss did so in 1931, and the Germans in 1932.

It was hoped that an annual British Ski Jumping Championships held during the same meeting as the Downhill race, and the Slalom which joined it in 1926, could replace the Challenge Cup. But as before the War, it proved difficult to entice all the best jumpers from far flung favourite haunts when there was no guarantee that conditions would be good enough. Ski jumps are often built next to villages to give them accessibility and a flat out-run, but none of the Bernese Oberland villages which were becoming important ski centres have the same altitude as St Moritz and Davos. Often their ski jumps are below the snow line, although conditions for downhill racing higher up may be good. Poor conditions and a paltry entry often made the event unworthy of its name.

In search of meaningful contests Alexander Keiller turned his attention to the Universities, with the result that when the 1928 Oxford and Cambridge match was held at St Moritz it consisted of four events for the first time, including ski jumping on the Julierschanze. For Colin Wyatt, a nineteen year old biologist at Caius, Cambridge, it was the perfect opportunity to show off his all-round form. The results were:

Downhill:	1. C. Wyatt (C)	2. G. Nixon (C)	3. J.Collins (O)
Slalom:	1. G Nixon (C)	2. D. Mackinnon (C)	3. T. Kagami (O)
Langlauf:	1. J.Dick (C)	2. C. Wyatt (C)	3. J. Huitfeldt (O)
Ski Jumping:	1. C. Wyatt (C)	2. J. Dick (O)	3.G. Nixon (O)

(Wyatt's length for three rounds: 28m, 30m and 32m)

Three weeks after this 1928 Varsity match which was held on 23 and 24 December, the 1929 British Championships were held on the same hill in mid-January. The undergrads, having gone home, there were only four competitors. Percy Legard with best rounds of 32m and 33m won from Heg Spence who cleared 30m and 32m. There were a number of notable absentees, but the student talent, not all of it from Oxbridge, was emerging nicely at a time when the International World Student Games had appeared on the calendar.

Alex Keiller was appointed referee for the second of these Games held at Davos in January 1930, and took with him a team of six representing the British Universities Ski Club (BUSC), yet another organisation of which he was President and Secretary. In all there were fifty competitors from the Universities or colleges of seven countries. Each man had three jumps, with the best two to count. Team results were to be decided by adding together the best four scores within each team.

There was a sensation after the first round which featured many falls, for the British team were in the lead. Wyatt stood at 43m for the second longest jump of the round, with Guy Nixon on 40m, John Dick on 38m and Richard Boord on 34m. In Britain's ski jumping history this was their finest hour, or maybe fifteen minutes, as Keiller found himself swamped with congratulations. The Bolganschanze was no picnic that day which was why so many of the original eighty-one entries had failed to turn up. Unfortunately as they started to throw a bit more into it in the second round Wyatt fell on 47m, and Nixon fell on 42m, but Howard Ford stood on 43m, Dick on 40m, and James Riddell on 39m.

In the final analysis the BUSC team finished third behind Austria and Germany, but ahead of the Swiss, Italians and French. The Swiss were a mixed collection. In J.de R. Keilland, a Norwegian at Zurich University, they had the winner of the Individual event, but the rest could hardly stay on their feet at all. John Dick, showing excellent style, came fourth, a fine performance which was totally unexpected. Howard Ford with 43m and 38m finished eighth, and Riddell with two jumps of 39m coming fifteenth. Such was the number who fell twice or even three times, that Nixon came twenty-first and Wyatt twenty-second. For Wyatt especially, after his brilliant start it was a terrible disappointment.

The real fireworks were provided by the Austrian brothers Helmut and Gustav Lantschner who each had two spectacular falls between 53m and 60m, none of which took too much out of them. Both became famous racers in the early days of international Downhill and Slalom racing, with Gustav winning the 1932 FIS World Championships downhill at Cortina.

The 1st Winter Olympic Games, Chamonix 1924

Although the Germans were not invited because of the War, the inaugural Winter Olympic Games at Chamonix in 1924 marked the first occasion when teams from the new skiing countries and the United States came together to take on the old. Hardly any of the European nations could even lay claim to twenty-five years of skiing history, and yet these first Olympics were almost held much earlier.

A proposal that winter sports be included at the Stockholm Olympics of 1912, or otherwise at a separate winter gathering was flatly rejected by the Swedes who felt it would threaten their Nordic Games which had been held every four years since 1901. The Germans, having been awarded the 1916 Games, were keen to stage a Winter Olympics at the Feldberg, but World War I made this irrelevant. The 1920 Games were

Jacob Tullin Thams jumping at the Chamonix Olympics 1924

granted to Belgium in honour of the suffering inflicted on its people during the War, but when the Games of 1924 went to France, the idea of a 'Winter Sports Festival' as it was called at first, was adopted.

Like the Swedes, the Norwegians were unenthusiastic, and Baron Pierre de Coubertin, the founder of the modern Olympic Games also had strong objections. On the other hand, most members of the International Ski Commission gave their support. The interruption of the War so soon after it had been founded, and the huge difference in standards between the Norwegians and the rest had meant that it was still far too early to arrange anything resembling a World Championships, but it was in the interests of the promotion of skiing that a start was made at some point, and if the International Olympic Commission was seen to take up such a task, so much the better.

The Ski Commission was wound up at its last meeting at Chamonix, and the International Ski Federation was established to take its place.

The Olympics at last gave the vastly superior Norwegians the incentive to take part without feeling obliged to give the opposition the sort of encouragement that they had commonly extended before. What happened at Klosters in 1922 was typical. Not unnaturally the locals were keen to catch up with neighbouring Davos and announced a magnificent International Ski Jumping competition on their new Selfrangaschanze. Three Norwegians had been induced to come, and there were a number of Germans and Austrians, and the best Swiss. After only one of the three rounds, two of the Norwegians retired in order to give their outclassed opponents the opportunity to fight for second and third places. Dagfinn Carlssen was left to win easily and in the process to make the first 50m jump seen in Europe. Afterwards all three staged the usual exhibition and coaching session to keep everyone happy.

Apart from a Military Patrol race won by the Swiss from the Finns, the skiing programme at Chamonix consisted of only three events: cross-country races of 50km and 18km, and the ski jumping. Within the last two however were contested a fourth individual event; that of the Nordic Combined.

Each nation was permitted to enter four men for each event, but the Norwegians sent just eight. Thorleif Haug, Toralf Stromstad and Johan Grottumsbraten proved quite good enough to come first, second and third in both the 50km and the Nordic

Jacob Tullin Thams, Narve Bonna and Einar Landvik at Chamonix 1924

Combined. Haug also won the 18km with Grottumsbraten second, to give himself three gold medals.

The final results of the ski jumping were not decided until fifty years later. In 1924 it appeared that the great Thorleif Haug had finished third, thus winning two medals at the same time; a bronze in the ski jumping, and a gold in the Nordic Combined. It also looked as if Tapani Niku of Finland who came third in the 18km race was the only man who had prevented the Norwegians from making a clean sweep of all twelve medals. But in 1974, long after Haug's death, there was an amendment. While looking back on those great days of his youth half a century before, Toralf Stromstad discovered an error in the computation of the scores. The Olympic Committee verified his findings and Haug was demoted to fourth place, while the Norwegian born Anders Haugen who had

Thorleif Haug

paid his own fare to Chamonix was moved up to third. At the age of eighty-three, Haugen felt unable to travel, so sent his daughter on his behalf to the special ceremony in Oslo where he was awarded Haug's medal. He remains the only American to win an Olympic medal for ski jumping.

The reassessment of the scores did not compromise the achievements of Jacob Tullin Thams from Drammen who became the first Olympic ski jumping champion with two jumps of 49m, and Narve Bonna who came second. In the exhibition which they gave afterwards, using a higher starting point, every Norwegian jumped over 50m, with Thams pulling off a 'monster' jump of 57·5m. It was a preview of the nasty accident at St Moritz four years later.

Inevitably the performances of the other twenty-three competitors from eight other countries suffered by comparison. Alexandre Girardbille from La Chaux de Fonds, Switzerland, showed nice style and his eighth place was the best of the Europeans. His compatriot Peter Schmidt managed 33·5m and almost fell at that. The Italians were graceful but poor with distance, and the French merely poor. The others were bad except for Haugan's American team mates who jumped with fierce determination although with atrocious style. They included John Carleton who had skied for Oxford in the inter-Varsity race of 1922. The trio of Mario Cavalha (Italy), Gilbert Ravanel (France) and Andrezn Krzeptowski (Poland) all tied on 32m for producing the shortest jumps, but in his second jump while competing in the Nordic Combined, A. Harbel (Hungary) cleared just 20m to set an Olympic 'record' which has stood the test of time.

For some reason or another the British did not receive the necessary invitation to send a team until November 1923 when it was too late to train one. Chris Mackintosh was certainly capable of beating many in the ski jumping, but at Oxford in early February, Olympic ski jumping was neither a possibility nor even a sporting priority. An athletics blue, he also gained a Scottish rugby cap as a three-quarter in the Scottish XV that lost to France in Paris in the spring.

And yet Mackintosh did jump in the Olympics that year after all. Only a few months later he returned to Paris for the Summer Games as Britain's representative in the Long Jump. Sprinting in and taking off with a burst of speed and power which none of the

Europeans had come up with at Chamonix, he cleared 6·92m to finish sixth. As if to prove the point his performance was indeed the best of the Europeans.

The event was notable in that William De Hart Hubbard (USA) who jumped 7·44m became the first black athlete to win an individual Olympic gold medal. Worthy as it was, Mackintosh's performance was eclipsed by his friend and fellow Scottish rugby international Eric Liddell who won the 400m by the proverbial 'street' after coming third in the 200m.

The triumphs of Liddell, and Harold Abrahams who won the 100m, are celebrated in the Oscar winning film *Chariots of Fire*, but none of the flabby throng of jubilant supporters mobbing the victorious Liddell bear much resemblance to Mackintosh.

The 2nd Winter Olympic Games, St Moritz 1928

The Julierschanze

After its foundation in Chamonix, the FIS set at once to organising an annual World Championships, starting at Johannisbad (Czechoslovakia) in 1925, then Lahti (Finland) in 1926, and Cortina d'Ampezzo (Italy) in 1927. The Norwegians who always considered their Holmenkollen to be the true World Championships, thought it all rather unnecessary and only sent a team to Lahti. There they were forced out of the first two places in both the cross country races of 30km and 50km by the host nation, but led by Thams and Grottumsbraten swept the boards in the ski jumping and the Nordic Combined.

Four years on from Chamonix, European standards had improved considerably. Cross country racing and ski jumping were still the only forms of ski competition, but they were jumping further on hills that were constantly being enlarged in a quest for new records that was becoming dangerous. It was sometimes the practice at local meets to rake up the snow on the take-off platform to form the sort of ramp that modern day aircraft carriers are fitted with.

Inevitably, such escalating ambitions to gain pre-eminence in the public eye would soon put them at odds with the Norwegians to whom the true test of the ski jumper has always been his style, and the distance that he could jump from a limited length of in-run leading down to a take-off which itself also sloped slightly downhill.

At St Moritz on a fine sunny afternoon on 18 February, as a huge crowd gathered around the Olympiaschanze in a high state of excitement in anticipation of a great contest, disputes and confusion immediately set in to cause a long delay to the irritation of all of them, and all because of a lack of procedure to decide on the starting point on the in-run.

The Norwegians had during the practice rounds over the previous week, and indeed prior to arriving in Switzerland at all, claimed that the Olympiaschanze would not be safe for their jumpers if they were to start from the top and go for the maximum distance for which each was capable. They did not however stipulate the amount of limit demanded, and did not go all out during practice.

Opponents pointed out that certain of the Swiss had consistently surpassed 65m in practice in perfect safety. Sepp Muhlbauer, a local of St Moritz who held the hill record with 70m, stated that in his opinion it was safe for longer distances.

Eventually it was decided that for the first round they should start from the 'junior platform', and from a higher point for the second round. After some scratchings due to injury, there were forty competitors from a record thirteen countries, including Austria, Canada and Japan with just one each.

At the end of the first round, Alf Andersen with 60m, was a clear leader from Sigmund Ruud who cleared 57·5m, and a thunderstorm of cheering broke out when the Swiss, Gerard Vuilleumier equalled this distance, and with slightly lower style marks than Ruud, put himself in third place just ahead of Rudolf Purkert of Czechoslovakia.

Decapitated! Such was the power with which Thams took off on his second jump at St Moritz 1928 that the phtographer was caught by surprise. Thams was anyway leaning forward, but moments later he crashed heavily.

The defending champion Jakob Tullin Thams disappointed with 56·5m to leave himself in fourth place, but the fourth Norwegian Hans Kleppen fell on the same distance.

The second round was started from a point some 5m further up the in-run, but still some way from the top. Andersen and Ruud, with jumps of 64m and 62·5m maintained their lead, but Vuilleumier fell at 62m. Purkert moved to third place, comfortably ahead of the two Swedes, Nilsson and Lundgren, who had left themselves with too much to do after modest first rounds.

All eyes were finally on Thams, who, desperate to recoup the deficit, was prepared to throw all caution to the wind as he had done so often at Holmenkollen. With all his power and superb timing he rose in the air in a manner entirely different from anything else seen in the afternoon, but then was suddenly in trouble. Alex Keiller who was in charge of telephone communications near the take-off, said that a sudden gust of west wind tipped him over in spite of his superb Vorlage. He crashed heavily at 73m, and for a moment it looked as if he was seriously hurt. He was rushed to the Morven Hut which doubled as the First Aid and Telephone Station, but the damage was only superficial, consisting of cuts and bruises. Still stunned when Keiller telephoned to enquire, he vent his frustrations on the incompetence of the organisers and their failure to ensure a safe competition.

It was Thams who won the hearts and admiration of the crowd that day. Had he stayed on his feet he would have set a new world record, but his accident did the sport a service in ensuring that nothing like it would ever happen again. It was clear to horrified Europeans that in future they would have to pay close attention to Norwegian opinion. It was a lesson for the IOC and FIS in particular.

Arnold Lunn commented: 'If Thams had started his run from the top he would have landed on the flat and probably have been killed, and I for one have never seen a more terrifying fall.' The performance of Sepp Muhlbauer served as an indicator of what would have happened. With 52m and 58m he came a creditable seventh, but these distances fell far short of his hill record of 70m which he had set earlier by starting from the top.

Thams was far from finished with the Olympics. He remained a force in ski jumping in Norway for a few more years, and won a silver medal at the Berlin Olympic Games of 1936 as a member of Norway's six man crew in the 8m sailing event. This was won by Italy, but Norway and Germany had to compete in a sail-off to decide second and third places. In the German boat was Alfred Krupp von Bohlen und Halbach the owner and director of the infamous Krupp armament works, who was convicted as a war criminal at the Nuremberg trials after World War II.

In winning that silver medal in Berlin twelve years after his gold medal at Chamonix, Tullin Thams became one of only three men who have won medals at Summer and Winter Olympics.

The Ruud brothers

In winning the silver medal at the 1928 Olympics, Sigmund Ruud not only announced his arrival on the world stage, but ushered in an era when he and his brothers, Birger and Asbjorn, almost completely dominated ski jumping up until World War II.

From the silver-mining town of Kongsberg, fifty-five miles south-west of Oslo, these three won the World Championships five times between them. The youngest, Asbjorn, who gained his triumph at Lahti (Finland) in 1938, was the only one who did not win an Olympic medal, but the family collection of two gold and two silver in ski jumping was not completed until the Games returned to St Moritz in 1948 for their resumption after the War.

Birger Ruud was thirty-six when he came to St Moritz as coach of the four man Norwegian jumping team which included his brother Asbjorn. He had won at Lake Placid in 1932, and again at Garmisch in 1936 when he even won the inaugural men's Downhill race as well, and no doubt he fancied himself as a reserve in the unlikely event of something going wrong with one of his charges. But the night before the competition, it was the weather that went wrong, and when he looked at the poor conditions he decided to compete in place of the less experienced George Thrane. Perhaps only he could have put himself under such pressure, but his confidence in himself paid off with the second place, and a silver medal just as Sigmund had won on the same hill, on the same occasion, twenty years before.

In Oslo in 1926, Sigmund became the first to jump 70m. In Switzerland it seemed that Bruno Trojani had gained this distinction at Pontresina, near St Moritz, where the locals had overtaken Klosters with their own latest and largest of jumping hills, but the date was found to fall a few days after Ruud's effort. Trojani, who somewhat disappointed at the Olympics, later became head of the ski school in Gstaad, but Reto Badrutt, the local boy who was left out of the Swiss team made his point by jumping 75m at Pontresina.

Such records as those set at Pontresina were of course achieved by making full use of an in-run that was far too long for men of the highest class, but the Europeans were getting carried away by the excitement of it all. Pontresina's reign at the 'top' lasted five years until 1931 when Davos reclaimed the spotlight. On the Bolganschanze which had been almost doubled in size, Sigmund Ruud jumped 81m. This made him the first to reach 80m, and three years later Birger became the first to jump 90m at Planica in Yugoslavia.

In between, Sigmund jumped 86m at Villars, Switzerland. Villars never became a ski jumping centre, but nature had endowed it with a perfect slope for Ruud's record making jump opposite the upper railway station at Bretaye.

Sigmund Ruud jumping 81 m at Davos 1931

Birger (left) and Asbjorn Ruud performing a double jump at Holmenkollen in 1954

Invited to Europe every winter, Sigmund and Birger simultaneously turned their attention to Downhill and Slalom racing which were rapidly gaining in popularity. In 1927, Arnold Lunn joined forces with Hannes Schneider of St Anton to run the first race for the Arlberg Kandahar, the world's senior international challenge cup decided on Downhill and Slalom, which is open to all comers. The FIS, having run World Championships for cross country and ski jumping since 1925, doubled its programme by introducing the same for Downhill and Slalom in 1931. These were held annually without a break until 1939.

The standard of Downhill skiing in Norway in 1930 was probably no better than in the Telemark of Sondre Norheim's day, seventy to eighty years before, and yet good ski jumpers possessed all the qualities necessary for the Downhill. It was one of Sigmund Ruud's great achievements that he was the first Norwegian to prove this, with the impact he made on the Alpine scene. He became a firm friend of the British, and did much to erode the hostile attitude of his fellow countrymen to these new forms of competitive skiing. He was also very helpful to British ski jumpers.

Competing in an early Arlberg Kandahar in Murren when racers had to choose their own line from the start to the finish, Sigmund made one of the most spectacular runs down the Schiltgrat that have ever been seen. 'Ruud's Line' is still commemorated there today, but a proper assessment of what his 'shuss' involved can only be gained after a good snowfall has recreated the conditions prevailing at the time.

Britain's over-50s

Ski jumping has always produced characters rich and rare, and in such a host, Colin Wyatt, Guy Nixon and Percy Legard occupy pedestals of their own. The three became Britain's first 50m ski jumpers at a time when the number of central Europeans who had reached that distance was not great. In the early 1930s equipment was still a bit unreliable. Boots offered limited support and there were far more falls than there are today. A jump of 50m put a man in a class of his own.

Totally unconventional and Bohemian, Wyatt gained fame as a skier, explorer and author, but notoriety in addition to further fame as an entomologist. For all his extraordinary talents and bravery, he owed a great deal to the enthusiasm and encouragement of Alex Keiller who ensured that he was able to use St Moritz as a base. With his flaming red hair which was far longer than anything previously seen in St Moritz, and his contagious high falsetto laugh, he could be seen and heard from almost every peak and bar in the Engadine.

Apart from his successes in two Varsity matches, Wyatt won the Downhill at the Anglo-Swiss Universities match in 1931. In Norway when the first two official Downhill and Slalom races were held in 1933, he won the Slalom in both. He also became the first British ski jumper to be admitted to the Holmenkollen competition, and in standing on two jumps of 36m and 38m he beat many of the central Europeans, and two of the Norwegians, neither of whom fell.

Between 1928 and 1931 Guy Nixon who also came to prominence while at Cambridge was Wyatt's team mate in many contests at every level. Captain Percy Legard, as he was then, joined them for whatever part of the winter the Army felt able to release him.

The most important event for which all three made up a British team was the 1931 FIS World Championships at Oberhof. It was the first time the

*Percy Legard jumping o[n]
the Julierschanze
St. Moritz*

Germans had staged one of the top events, and seventy-three competitors were entered for the Special Jumping on the new Hindenbergschanze. The local band was brought in, and as each jumper appeared at the start he was greeted with a lusty rendition of some chosen item from his country's musical heritage. For the last, and probably the only time before Hitler came to power, a rousing ' Britannia Rules the Waves' rose to the skies above Bavaria, as Wyatt appeared. For Nixon the band struck up 'Home Sweet Home', but for Percy there was something of a mix-up as musicians fumbled with their sheets, and none of the Brits could make out what it was. Percy himself was a rumbustuous drummer who later appeared on Yorkshire TV, and in many an Alpine ballroom and disco, but he was concentrating on the job that stretched out far below. The results were as follows:

1. Birger Ruud (Norway)	56·5m	58m	236·0 points
2. Fritz Kaufmann (Switz)	57	56	228·8
3. Sven Ericksson (Sweden)	56	55·5	227
40 Colin Wyatt	43	46	
42. Percy Legard	42	46	
60. Guy Nixon	44(F)	49	

Fritz Kaufmann of Grindelwald achieved much the best result by a central European so far at this topmost level. Birger Ruud gained the first of his many World and Olympic titles. Three of his team mates, including his brother Sigmund, came fourth, fifth and sixth, but the other two both fell once, and finished forty-ninth and fifty-second. Had Guy Nixon not fallen on his first jump he would have finished in the top half.

Many of the same competitors, including Legard and Nixon were also among the seventy-one entrants for the Nordic Combined. Nixon had very little experience of the langlauf but was anxious to have another go at the jumping hill. Legard had not had enough training.

The Olympic champion Johan Grottumsbraten won the 17km langlauf in 1hr 23min. Legard came fifty-eighth in 1hr 50min, and Nixon sixty-first in 2hr 2min. After many falls which kept the leader board changing, the jumping was won by Sverre Kolterud (Norway) who cleared 56m and 55m. Birger Ruud and Fritz Kaufmann both went further, but both had falls which set them back somewhat. To his great credit Guy Nixon stood twice on 46·5m and 50m. So far as distance was concerned he was eleventh, but his style set him back to twenty-second. Only forty-seven of the seventy-one competitors finished both sections. Grottumsbraten won easily from Kolterud. Nixon came thirty-fourth, with Legard, after some disappointing jumping, forty-third.

The winter of 1930/31 was memorable for much more. Nixon won the third Varsity ski jumping match on 23 December. On 10 January the best ever British Championships was won by Wyatt (46m and 46m) from Legard (45m and 43m) and nine others. It was held in conjunction with an open Swiss event on the Jungfrauschanze at Wengen. Wyatt was a brilliant second behind Adolf Rubi who was twice Swiss champion, and Legard fourth just ahead of the great Fritz Kaufmann who did 52m after a fall on his first jump.

Nixon also had a fall, but then went on to gain a very satisfactory twelfth place out of forty-four in the Swiss Championships at Adelboden. This was still open to non-Swiss nationals until 1934. Wyatt meanwhile returned to St Moritz for the Morven Cup, the most important of the local competitions, on the Olympiaschanze. He had been seriously injured there the previous year, but proved his nerve had not been affected when he raised his British record to 57·5m.

After the World Championships, Legard had to return to his unit in England, but Nixon and Wyatt joined the many whose next destination was Davos for the latest and greatest spectacular on that soaring white eminence of a status symbol, the Bolganschanze. After yet another enlargement it was once again the largest ski jumping hill in the world. For the competition, a comparatively short in-run was employed, and Kaufmann with three jumps of 60m, 66m and 62m won from Sigmund Ruud whose best was 62m. The real thrills began immediately afterwards. Ruud decided to go all out from a longer in-run and set a new world record of 81m. Nixon followed him and cleared 62m to eclipse Wyatt's record set only two weeks before. It has to be born in mind however that Wyatt's record was set under competitive conditions and not 'ausser Konkurrenz'.

The 3rd Winter Olympics at Lake Placid in 1932 were but a distant mirage for Nixon and Wyatt, but less of a frustration for Legard for whom the Modern Pentathlon at the Summer Olympics at Los Angeles six months later proved to be a rewarding alternative. Furthermore, by the time his two friends had retired from jumping, Percy became the first British ski jumper to take flight in a Winter Olympics when he competed in the Nordic Combined at Garmisch in 1936.

Percy Legard was born of an English father and a Swedish mother whose family

...er advertising the ...ord/Cambridge match ...ember 1928

The British team at the World Championships 1931.
(Left to right) *Guy Nixon, Colin Wyatt, Percy Legard*

included some keen skiers. His cousin, the clergyman Percy Hallencreutz was Chairman of the Organising Committee when the World Alpine Ski Championships were held at Are, Sweden, in 1954. In his role of priest he also presided over special services for the athletes taking part.

Percy spent his first fifteen years in Sweden where he learnt his Nordic skiing. He then attended Cheltenham College for two years before going to Sandhurst from where he was commissioned into the Fifth Royal Inniskilling Dragoon Guards. The question that arises at this point is whether Eddie Edwards was the first Olympic ski jumper from Cheltenham, or merely the second?! As the best sports club in the world, the British Army provided Percy with considerable opportunity to extend his talents into other fields, and he went on to represent Great Britain in the Modern Pentathlon in the two summer Olympic Games of 1932 and 1936, as well as the Nordic Combined in 1936.

The Bolganschanze at Davos on 24 February 1931 when Sigmund Ruud became the first man to jump 80m, clearing 81m. Guy Nixon jumped 62m to set a British record which lasted fifty-six years

There was even a fourth Olympic appearance in the Winter Pentathlon which was included as an experiment in the 1948 Winter Olympics at St Moritz, but never repeated. Performances were poor and no records were kept. Everyone had had a tough time in the War including Percy himself who later retired as a Lt Colonel. Even if we disregard the Slalom which formed one part of that Winter Pentathlon, Percy participated in more Olympic sports than anyone else: running, riding swimming, fencing, shooting, langlaufing and jumping. (See also 4th Winter Olympics.)

Guy Nixon sadly disappeared during the War, but Colin Wyatt survived, and combined a distinguished career as an entomologist who specialised in butterflies, with that as a writer on the more remote and little explored mountain ranges of the world. He spent most of 1949 and 1950 in the Atlas Mountains of Morocco, and it was in those parts that he gained enduring fame in two very different fields.

As a member of the Swiss Alpine Club, it was he who suggested the Swiss expedition to the High Atlas in 1950. In the course of this Wyatt and his Swiss friends made the first ski ascent of the Toubkal (4,165m) the highest peak in the massif, which looks down upon Marrakesh. In the same year, travelling by himself, he made the first ski crossing of the Goun Massif (4,071m) in the same range. Many of his beautiful photographs taken in these and other ranges round the world feature in his book *The Call of the Mountains* published in 1953.

Below the peaks of the Atlas he spent many months living in a tent studying the butterflies, and his observations led to a number of discoveries. One such was the life cycle of the species *Maurus vogeli*, and the larval association of that species with ants.

To his friends in the bars of the Engadine who recalled his pre-War triumphs as a Dowhill and Slalom racer in Norway, and his fine performance at Holmenkollen, it all seemed as if such enlightenment for mankind would earn Colin a further summons to Scandinavia, this time to Stockholm for the award of the Nobel Prize. Many were aware however that he had been in the doghouse with the scientific community for some years.

On 1 May 1947 Wyatt appeared at the West Ham Magistrates Court in London and pleaded guilty to a charge arising from the theft of 1,600 Lycaenid butterflies from museums in Sydney and Melbourne. He was fined £100. That was apparently not the only theft he had carried out, for back in 1930 a total of 279 Colias and Parnassius butterflies had disappeared from the Natural History Museum in South Kensington, and there had been strong circumstantial evidence that Wyatt had been responsible. After seventeen years these specimens were returned to the Natural History Museum shortly before he entered the dock at West Ham. The huge Australian collection was sent home too.

Colin Wyatt was killed in an air crash in Guatemala in 1975. He was sixty-six, and his butterfly collections were sold to the Staatliche Museum fur Naturkunde in Karlsruhe in Germany. Ski jumpers passing through on their way to the Feldberg, and the big World Cup events at Neustadt and Hinterzarten will find that the collections include many brightly coloured V-style fliers that nature created long before the ski jumpers pulled on their own coloured suits and attempted to copy them.

The girls reflect on the days of the 'upright young men'

The 3rd Winter Olympic Games, Lake Placid 1932

Attendance at the 3rd Winter Olympics at Lake Placid, a town of less than 4,000 in New York State, was affected to some extent by the Depression. The prospect of a rough mid-winter crossing of the Atlantic to America in the midst of Prohibition also served to discourage, but most of the European nations sent individuals to represent them in something. They were greeted on arrival by dreadful weather which was always a possibility for Lake Placid is situated at only 568m.

The skiing programme was still restricted to the Nordic events, but such was the lack of snow that downhill races would have been cancelled anyway. Trucks had to be sent to Canada to bring in snow for the cross country courses, and the ski jumpers were soaked as they finished up in a pool of water.

Sweden gained the first two places in the shorter 15km race, and Finland the first two places in the 50km. The Norwegians failed to guess the best wax combinations, but they maintained their domination of the ski jumping with the first three places, and the Nordic Combined with a clean sweep of the first four.

Not often has the weather been known to co-operate helpfully with the festival of the Winter Olympics, but in 1932 it was at its worst, and it was something that the winner Birger Ruud recalled to himself sixteen years later when the Fohn came down at St Moritz in 1948, and when as coach of the Norwegian team he decided to substitute himself in place of one of his less experienced charges. Birger won very narrowly at Lake Placid from his friend Hans Beck who had a large lead after the first round, but disappointed on the second. Like the Ruud brothers, Beck was from Kongsberg, and all three were brought up together. The gap in class between them and the central Europeans was reduced by the fine performance of Fritz Kaufmann of Grindelwald who managed to gain sixth place just ahead of Sigmund Ruud.

Johann Grottumsbraten again won the Nordic Combination, ending his participation in the first three Winter Olympics with three gold medals, one silver and two bronze.

The 4th Winter Olympics, Garmisch-Partenkirchen, 1936

The IOC's newly developed custom of awarding the Summer and Winter Games to the same country as much as five years ahead resulted in the unfortunate choice of Germany for 1936 by which time Hitler and the Nazi Party had come to power. Jews in various countries called for a boycott of the Games, and in the United States a proposal for a boycott was only narrowly defeated.

An alternative People's Olympics were scheduled for Barcelona, but were cancelled at the last moment because of the outbreak of the Spanish Civil War, and so Berlin was left to stage the Summer Games without losing many of the participating nations and their athletes to an alternative which might have had greater appeal.

At Garmisch Downhill and Slalom races were included for the first time in a Winter Olympics, but due to the amateur status that was required for all athletes by IOC rules, ski instructors were not permitted in these or any other competition. The FIS did not recognise these Alpine events at Garmisch as the equivalent of a true World Championships, and therefore staged a separate Alpine World Championships at nearby Innsbruck after the Games.

Birger Ruud's extraordinary achievement of winning the Downhill race, as well as the ski jumping for the second time, has to be seen in the light of the absence of the men who would normally have been his chief rivals. There is no doubt at all however that he was among the best in the Downhill for he had come fourth in the World Championships at Murren in 1935, and in order to gain every opportunity to train over the Zugspitze course he went to live in Garmisch before the snows fell. It was greatly to his credit that instead of resting on his laurels after Garmisch, he went on to Innsbruck. In coming fourth in the Downhill, as he had done at Murren the year before, he beat all the Austrians, and lost only to the Swiss pair of Rudolf Rominger and Heinz von Allmen, and Sertorelli of Italy.

For the British, the thrilling progress of their ice hockey team at Garmisch provided ever increasing excitement. In winning five of their seven matches and drawing the other two, the team gained their country's first gold medal at a Winter Olympics.

In the women's Downhill and Slalom, Jeanette Kessler and Evie Pinching came eighth and ninth in the Combined results to register the best British performances in the skiing. For the first and only time in the Olympics, Britain had an entrant in the Nordic Combination which was decided on an 18km cross-country race and ski jumping. The table at the bottom of the page details Percy Legard's performance in coming forty-fifth out of fifty-one.

Using borrowed skis, Percy produced an astonishing second jump of 44m which was only 1m less than that of the gold medallist Oddbjorn Hagen, but in the cross-country he disappointed. Although he had done all he possibly could to prepare himself through his cross-country running in the Army, it was lack of training on the snow that was to blame. He also lacked the long experience of the Scandinavians in the finer arts of waxing. For these reasons Percy's sporting career shows that a man who turns himself into a runner to be reckoned with, through hard training on roads and across country, does not necessarily make himself a top class cross-country skier.

In finishing eighth out of twenty-five in the Modern Pentathlon at the Summer Olympics at Los Angles in 1932, Percy came first in the cross-country race. There was no gold medal for this magnificent effort unfortunately, for it was just one event of five. Six months after Garmisch, Hitler presided over the opening of the Summer Olympics in Berlin, and Percy was again able to take a look at the Fuhrer from the vantage point of the march-past.

In later life when surrounded, as he often was, by pretty girls and bottles of Fendant, Percy liked to recall how on that second occasion he 'gave the bastard a V-sign!' A great entertainer, Percy was there to take part in his second Olympic Modern Pentathlon. He finished nineteenth out of forty-two, and was still good enough to come fourth in the cross-country run.

The Nordic Combination at Garmisch-Partenkirchen, 1936

The Nordic Combination at the 1936 Olympics attracted fifty-one competitors from sixteen nations, and was held on 13 February. These figures show how Percy Legard's performances compared with those of the top four who were all Scandinavians, and Stanislav Marusarz of Poland who came seventh. A year earlier Marusarz jumped 97m at Planica to become the world record holder for a brief spell. Three days after the Nordic Combination, Marusarz and Valonen also competed in the Special Jumping, finishing fifth and sixth.

| | | | 18km | | Ski Jumps | | | Total |
			Time	Points	Distances		Points	Points
1.	Oddbjorn Hagen	Nor	1:15:33	240·0	41·0	45·0	190·3	430·3
2.	Olaf Haffsbraken	Nor	1:17:37	227·8	46·0	44·5	192·0	419·8
3.	Sverre Brodahl	Nor	1:18:01	225·5	45·0	45·5	182·6	408·1
4.	Lauri Valonen	Fin	1:26:34	178·6	51·0	53·5	222·6	401·2
7.	Stanislav Marusarz	Pol	1:25:27	183·5	47·5	48·5	208·9	393·3
45.	Percy Legard	GB	1:47:47	76·8	39·0	44·0	171·5	248·3

A sudden decline as downhill runs are opened up

Alex Keiller could feel well pleased with the results that his British team achieved in the few years they had together, but quite suddenly ski jumping started to go into decline in the same Alpine centres which had adopted the sport so enthusiastically before World War I. It was the excitement of ski jumping which provided the necessary impetus for so many of them.

In the 1930s as more mountain railways and ski lift systems were installed, the joys of the Downhill Only form of skiing became more easily accessible. Nowhere was the decline more dramatic than at Davos. In 1933, just two years after Sigmund Ruud became the first man to jump 80m on the newly enlarged Bolganschanze, the Parsennbahn was opened, and what Edward Richardson described as 'by far the best tour I have ever made' could easily be done two or three times in a day.

The decline came about not because everyone wanted to abandon the ski jumps altogether, but because too many were enticed away for too much of the time. The problem for ski jumpers has always been that unless they gather in sufficient numbers, they will either have to spend too long preparing a hill, or they will find it not worth the trouble to prepare it at all. It generally takes ten men half a day to get a 30m hill ready after a snowfall, and then it may snow again, which of course is what the powder enthusiast wants. Far better it was to go off and enjoy it, instead of treading it in.

For the chap on holiday who was keen to give it a go if the hill was brought into use, further complications later arose with changes in the design of ski boots. Until about 1960 all ski boots had a groove around the back of the heel to accommodate the cable binding which was still in common use for Alpine skiing. Very importantly the cable could be adjusted to allow the heel to lift if one wanted to jump or go touring. It was a binding for all forms of skiing. Around this time the cable binding was replaced by new heel release systems for downhill skiing, and ski boots were redesigned to fit into them. The heel groove disappeared, and it was no longer possible to fit these boots to the cable bindings on a pair of jumping skis.

Naturally enough all the sports shops in the large Alpine centres remained geared to the needs of the downhillers, and nowadays as it has turned out, to the snowboarders. For the large numbers of British, and others like them who visit these places, ski jumping is no longer possible. And yet interest in ski jumping is still strong. In Wengen for very many years the local club has regularly employed a work force to prepare a small 30m hill for night ski jumping competitions under floodlights. These shows attract large numbers of paying spectators, but the hearty young men who show up to compete, often on an icy hill, do so with bulky and inflexible Alpine ski boots with heels fixed firmly to downhill or even slalom skis. It is a rough way of doing it, but they are fine skiers and it is not a problem. In Lauberhorn week 1966 the great French racer Jean Claud Killy revealed all by dropping his pants in the moment of take-off. They were restored on landing, but the following morning the local photographer had a queue of customers asking for enlargements.

Among the pre-War fixtures that disappeared was the Oxford and Cambridge ski jumping match. Colin Wyatt won in 1928 and 1929, and Guy Nixon in 1930. There was then a long interlude before it was held for the fourth and final time in Sestrierre in Italy in 1938. David Bradley, also of Cambridge, who won on that last occasion, had jumped 50m back home in New England.

In its short life it attracted every available British visitor, and many others, to the dizzy excitement at the hill, and it was a tragedy that its very special role in providing eccentrics with a launch pad in life was never re-established.

World records: the first 100 metres

1809	Olaf Rye	9·5m	near Gamle Aker church
1860	Sondre Norheim	30m	Morgedal, Telemark
1891	Mikkel Hemmestveit	31m	Red Wing, Minnesota
1893	Torjus Hemmestveit	32m	Red Wing, Minnesota

(Torjus set his record in the 'New World'.
The Solbergbakken first used in 1897, enabled 'Old World' records to be set.)

1897	Sven Sollid	31·5m	Solbergbakken
	Cato Aall	31·5m	Solbergbakken
1899	Asbjorn Nilssen	32·5m	Solbergbakken
	Morten Hansen	32·5m	Solbergbakken
1900	Olaf Tandberg	35m	Solbergbakken
1902	Paul Nesjo (aged 18)	39m	Trondheim
	Nils Gjestvang	40·5m	Modum
1906	Harald Smith	45m	Davos, Switzerland
1909	Harald Smith	48m	Davos
1915	Amble Amundsen	54m	Oslo
1916	Ragnar Omtvedt (Chicago)	58·5m	Steamboat Springs, Colorado
1918	Henry Hall (Michigan)	61·5m	Steamboat Springs
1925	Anders Haugen	64m	Steamboat Springs
1926	Dagfinn Carlssen	65m	Pontresina, Switzerland
	Sigmund Ruud	70m	Oslo
1928	Reto Badrutt	75m	Pontresina, Switzerland
1931	Sigmund Ruud	81m	Davos
1933	Sigmund Ruud	86m	Villars, Switzerland
1934	Sigmund Ruud	87·5m	Planica, Yugoslavia
	Birger Rund	92m	Planica
1935	Reidar Andersen	93m	Planica
	Stanislav Marusarz (Poland)	97m	Planica
	Reidar Andersen	99m	Planica
	Franz Kainersdorfer (Swiss)	99m	Ponte di Legno, Italy
1936	Sepp Bradl (Austria)	101m	Planica

CHAPTER IV

TOWARDS 2000

The quest for records

At Planica, Yugoslavia, the new 'monster' jump which was made ready for its opening in 1934 provided towering evidence of ever growing expectations of new records. Although it enabled Birger Ruud to become the first man to jump 90m, the Norwegian authorities were not entirely pleased for the jump had been specially designed to make possible much longer jumps than hitherto.

Nikolai Oestgaard, the Norwegian President of the FIS strongly disapproved, and at his instigation, the FIS in 1936 passed a rule that start licences would be refused for competitors on hills that had a critical point of more than 80m.

The Planica management who had just completed an enlargement of the jump, decided nevertheless to go ahead with a competition which they had scheduled for later that year. Jumpers from a number of countries agreed to compete, but the Norwegians, under pressure from their own authorities, refused. It was the first major competition without them, and on 18 March 1936, the eighteen year-old Austrian, Sepp Bradl, made ski jumping history by becoming the first to jump 100m. Stanko Bloudec, the engineer who had designed the jump, had the right words for it, when he exclaimed: 'That was no longer ski jumping. That was ski flying!'

On these very long flights the jumper has time in the air to experiment with his aerodynamic position until he suddenly gets the feeling that he is gliding. It is this aerodynamic position, rather than the power and timing at take-off, which is decisive in achieving distance.

The scene at Villars in February 1933 when Sigmud Ruud set a new world record of 86m

The correct aerodynamic position, while it can only be properly learnt on very large jumps, is also of great importance on jumps of normal size. The Norwegians were for a long time discouraged from competing on these very large hills, so that jumpers from other countries came to surpass them in acquiring the most effective aerodynamic style, and the Norwegians lost their hegemony even on small hills. In the six Winter Olympics between 1924 and 1952 the Norwegians won all six gold medals for ski jumping, five of the silver medals and four of the bronze. In 1956 and 1960 they did not win any medals for jumping at all.

Planica was not the only monster jump at this point for the Italians had also decided to get a share of the action by building their version at Ponte di Legno in the province of Brescia. This was very nearly the scene of the first 100m jump, for the Swiss champion, Franz Kainersdorfer, cleared 99m there in 1935.

The contours of the mountainside at Planica allowed for a great deal of natural enlargement of the jumping hill, and it was while Yugoslavia was under German occupation in 1940 that the first extension was carried out to enable the Nazi propaganda machine to boast a spectacular succession of five new records, each set by the master race. One of the three jumpers involved was an Austrian, Franz Maier, but the sequence ended with Rudolf Gehring's 112m which remained the record until Fritz Tschanen of Adelboden jumped 120m in 1948.

In 1949 a hill to make even longer jumps possible was completed at Oberstdorf in Bavaria. It had a critical point of 120m, and the starting point at the top of the tower rose to 161m above the bottom. At first the FIS refused to sanction it, but in the end they agreed that 'exceptionally' a competition could be held there in 1950. The Oberstdorf authorities billed this as an 'International Ski Flying Week'. It started on 26 February with Andreas Dascher of Davos, the new Swiss champion, jumping 121m. He had to be content with a national record, as did Willy Gantschnigg of Austria who followed two days later with 124m. Another two days on, the West German, Sepp Weiler, equalled the record with 127m, and then on the final day, 1 March, the Swede, Dan Netzell, jumped 135m.

Sixty thousand spectators turned up when the week was repeated in 1952. A nineteen year-old Finn, Tauno Luiro, who had never jumped more than 90·5m missed the first day because his skis had not arrived. They turned up next day and he was able to jump four times. He began with 111m and 119m, standing both times. Then came a fall, but without damage, after landing at 131m, and he finished very steadily on 132m. Some were less fortunate. Toni Brutscher came down head first at 129, but he escaped injury for the blow was glancing and not direct. Far more serious were the spinal injuries suffered by Bruno da Col of Italy. After a faulty take-off, a gust of wind turned him upside down and twisted him around so that he landed head first and backwards.

Later the following day Tauno Luiro stood at the top of the tower, barely visible to the crowd spread about far below, and there he waited and continued to wait. He had seen da Col's terrible fall and people wondered whether he had lost his nerve, for the wind balloons and limp flags showed no sign of movement, and it seemed a good time to jump. But Luiro was watching for evidence of upward wind which could give him extra distance, although upward draughts often turn sideways very suddenly. After fifteen minutes he set off and jumped. Later people said that it seemed he would never land; they also said that when he had reached about 125m he seemed to get extra carry. Either it was the updraught, or he managed to make a slight adjustment to his flight position. He landed at 139m deep in the curve (R2 in the charts) and absorbed the weight of his landing by the usual method of dropping into a telemark position, his rear knee almost touching his ski.

After such a long wait, the tension in the crowd was suddenly released and people stormed across the palisades to lift the new hero into the air. Sadly Tauno Luiro was a diabetic. He had been taking insulin injections throughout this time, but when he returned to Oberstdorf in 1952 he was not at all his former ebullient self. Back home in Rovaniemi on the edge of the Arctic Circle, he contacted tuberculosis, and died in 1954. It is said that he died happy in the belief that, mortal himself, his record was eternal. In fact his record stood for ten years which is itself a record.

In 1961 Tauno Luiro's record was surpassed by Josef Slibar of Yugoslavia on the same hill. The Norwegians came to accept ski flying and built a monster jump of their own at Vikersund, 30km from Oslo. There Bjorn Wirkola set a new world record of 146m in 1966. His compatriot Lars Grini became the first to reach 150m at Oberstdorf the following year.

The FIS also came to accept ski flying, and in 1972 inaugurated a biennial World Ski Flying Championships. They had failed to prevent record breaking, but they did slow down the process. But for them, even larger jumps would have been built before enough was understood about their design requirements, and the safety record of the sport could have been tarnished.

Plastic matting and growth in Eastern Europe

Garmisch during the Four Hills competition

It was on a 30m hill at Neustadt, the birthplace of German ski jumping, that plastic matting was first tried out on a jumping hill in 1959. The long strands of 'thatch' (or 'spaghetti') all pointing downhill proved to be a great success and it was not long before this new idea was taken up far and wide, especially in Eastern Europe where Alpine skiing barely exists, and Japan.

Ski jumping could now be practised in summer with no more preparation than a spray of water over the plastic, and when global warming started to manifest itself it was very often the only form of skiing available. In the space of only twelve years between 1960 and 1972, East Germany, the Soviet Union, Czechoslovakia, Poland and Japan all managed to produce at least one Olympic ski jumping champion.

Up until 1956 the only winners had been Norwegians and Finns, but success on such a widening scale was made possible by the decision of the IOC in 1964 to include a 90m competition in the Olympics in addition to the usual 70m event. This gave competitors a second chance to win medals in a sport where a sudden gust of wind or a split second mistake can ruin a performance, but the results over those years were an indication of the sport's healthy expansion which brought the Scandinavian monopoly to an end.

Some developments were less than healthy. In the early 1950s state-trained athletes from the Soviet Union and East Germany began to make an impact in cross country races at major FIS and Olympic championships. Emblazoned with the letters CCCP and DDR, and constantly guarded by their porridge-faced minders from the KGB, these men and 'women' were an unwelcome intrusion into the ski fraternity. By the late 1950s they started to have some success in ski jumping, and the Communist sports authorities were quick to start a programme of plastic hill construction. By the mid-1960s they were up among the best in both jumping and the Nordic combined.

Poland has never produced any skiers of consequence in either cross country or Alpine, and yet their ski jumpers sometimes reach the heights. Wojciech Fortuna was an outstanding Olympic champion on the Large Hill in 1972. He trained all through the year on snow and plastic, as did Adam Malysz who became World Champion in the winter of 2000/01.

The Czech and Slovak Republics which formerly made up Czechoslovakia have a certain amount of Alpine skiing, but as with Poland, success at the top level has come in the Nordic events. Skiing came early to Bohemia at much the same time as it did to the Black Forest, and quite often the cross country team is a force to be reckoned with. A remarkable early success came up when Rudolf Purkert came third in the ski jumping at the second Winter Olympics in 1928. To beat all but two of the Scandinavians was not part of the script. Forty years later Jiri Raska won gold and silver medals at Grenoble in 1968, and countless many fine jumpers have followed him ever since.

The most important plastic ski jump centre is at Frenstat pod Radhostem in North Moravia, some 300km east of Prague. This contains five hills of all sizes up to a K90

Summer ski jumping at Predazzo, Italy

Veikko Kankkonen (Finland) at Holmenkollen in 1964

which is the venue every year for one of the major internationals on the summer circuit. It is an outstanding success story, for ski jumps have brought visitors and prestige, and even during the years under Communism other very attractive developments followed. Until the dramatic events in the autumn of 1989, Frenstat was the base for the Soviet Union's 31st Tank Regiment which occupied what was the town's dominant feature, a dreary military barracks where the hapless Russian soldiers were not even allowed out to watch the ski jumping. The abrupt manner in which they pulled out and went home in a succession of huge convoys was cause for national rejoicing.

Leningrad and Moscow were two of the first cities to build artificial ski jumps in the early 1960s. The two Moscow jumps of K40 and K70 are fairly centrally located on a steep section of Gorky Park that rises from near the river to the flat expanses opposite the Lomonosov University. The structures can be seen from east of the river for some distance.

In Scandinavia and Western Europe the establishment of these centres reached a peak in the 1980s and has since tailed off. In West Germany many are located far from the main ski areas in such places as the Sauerland hills in the north, and Rastbuckle/Breitenberg in the south-east. Since amalgamation with East Germany they have had over forty of them. The Austrians have also invested heavily, the two large hills at Stams where there is a special school for the best young skiers being of special importance. Switzerland, Italy and France each have major centres at Kandersteg, Predazzo and Courchevel. The last mentioned was constructed for the 1992 Olympics.

While plastic matting has always proved a suitable material for landing slopes, it has long been replaced, on all but the smallest hills, by tracks of ceramic tiles. Some versions incorporate heating cables to keep the surfaces of these tracks (or 'tram lines') ice free so that they can be used in winters of poor snow.

The rise of the Japanese

During the Meiji period (1876-1912) which coincided with the introduction of skiing into central Europe, Japan started to open up to the outside world, and almost all of today's popular sports have been introduced since that time.

An Austrian army officer Theodore von Lerch took his skis with him when he went off to visit the Japanese army in the winter of 1910/11. Gaishi Nagaoka, the commanding officer of the 13th Division at Takada, 200m north of Tokyo, had already paid a visit to central Europe, and had been able to observe skiers for himself. Realising that skiing had its usefulness for the military, as well as the potential to become a popular sport, he was keen to get it started in his homeland. With the arrival of von Lerch he had a man who could help and advise, and he got moving. Local carpenters and the Tanaka ironworks were contracted to turn out skis and bindings, and before the winter was over the 13th Division was not only teaching itself, but the local people as well.

More Austrians, including Hannes Schneider, came to teach after World Wart I, and once again it was ski jumping which took hold of the peoples' attention. Small and agile, they were being shown a sport for which they were naturally suited. Amazingly, they were able to send a ski jumper to the 2nd Winter Olympics at St Moritz in 1928. Motchiko Ban finished last, but all learning curves start from the bottom, and in Japan's case their dedication took them all the way to the very top. Spectacular success was achieved when they hosted the Winter Olympics for the first time in 1972, but if home ground gave a certain advantage, and it appeared at the time to be something of a one-off, this was no longer the case when they again hosted the Olympics in 1998. By then Japan was consistently in the front rank, not just in ski jumping, but in the Nordic combined also.

The clean sweep of the medals in the 70m ski jumping at Sapporo in 1972 provided a dramatic illustration of what could be achieved with plastic matting. The hills built for the Games were covered to provide training for their team throughout the summer of 1971. It has since been common practice for host nations to do this, but matting is now in almost universal use. The real advantage comes with providing the ski jumper with familiarity with wind behaviour on the hills concerned. Nowadays, with 'V-style' and larger hills, wind is more than ever an influential factor in determining a jumper's performance.

The excitement was particularly great at Sapporo on 6 February 1972 because the leading Japanese jumper, the twenty-eight year-old Yukio Kasaya was a hometown boy from Japan's northernmost island of Hokkaido, where the Games were being held. His team mates, Akitsugu Konno and Seiji Aochi, were also from Hokkaido. Kasaya had emerged as favourite with the bookmakers having pulled off an astonishing treble at the Four Hills tournament which had finished five weeks earlier, winning at Oberstdorf, Garmisch and Innsbruck. Consequently the hopes of a whole nation anxious for a first gold medal at a Winter Olympics rested upon him, and among the crowd of 100,000 were his old schoolfriends from Yoichimachi High School waving the school flag.

Despite the enormous pressure, Kasaya produced the best jump of each round. While the nation rejoiced over the stunning Japanese sweep, Kasaya, who had made 10,000 jumps since he was aged eleven, reminded the press of his personal motto: 'Challenge not your rivals, but yourself.' Nine days later when the Games concluded with the 90m Ski Jumping, the new idols were not so successful. Kasaya's 106m was the third best of the first round, but a second round jump of 85m pulled him back to seventh place.

Twenty years later it started to become apparent that the ski jumpers of Japan were going to be the chief beneficiaries of the 'V-style' revolution. Small and slim, their body profiles seemed ideally suited aerodynamically. Noriaki Kasai became the first Japanese since Kasaya to win one of the Four Hills, and as the technique became more refined, success at the top level became routine. If they failed to win an individual event, they would win the team jumping or the Nordic combined instead.

In 1998 the Winter Olympics returned to Japan to be staged at Nagano in the middle of Honshu, and once again triumphs in the ski jumping were a cause for national celebration, but this time even more so. In Kazuyoshi Funaki the nation had a clear favourite to win, just as they had in Kasaya twenty-six years before. And like Kasaya, Funaki had won the same three Four Hills competitions just a few weeks earlier. Funaki did not let them down. After coming second to the Finn, Jari Soininen, in the 90m event, he went on to beat Soininen to the gold medal on the 120m hill, with Masahiko Harada third. Afterwards Funaki and Harada linked up with two other team mates to win the Team Jumping on the 120m hill, and it was only in the Nordic Combined that they came undone.

The V-style and the modern era

In Sweden the general rule that a nation's sporting pursuits are governed by its geography and climate does not always apply. Since World War II the Swedes have produced many outstanding cross country skiers. They also turn out tennis champions of the highest class, but their ski jumpers have lagged behind those of Norway and Finland by a distance.

It was nevertheless a red-headed Swedish jumper, Jan Boklov, who was responsible for introducing the so-called 'V-style' method which swiftly and decisively changed the face of the sport between 1989 and 1992, and led to a major revision of the sizes of hills used for major competitions.

A catamaran's evening cruise

Matti Nykanen

In March 1988 Boklov gave a big indication of what was to come when he finished second behind the newly crowned Olympic champion Matti Nykanen at Lahti. It was the first time a Swede had gained a place on a podium since the annual World Cup ski jumping series was begun in the winter of 1979/80, and was even more remarkable because some judges deducted points for reasons that his unconventional style looked neither safe nor attractive.

Boklov did not leave anyone long in doubt that his method was effective. A year later he emerged a World Cup winner having won five of the twenty rounds that comprised the series in the winter of 1988/89. His first two victories came at Lake Placid (US) and Sapporo (Japan) and it was no wonder that ski jumpers everywhere, especially among the young, started to imitate him. The Japanese, analytical as ever, found that it suited their slim physiques perfectly, but controversy raged with traditionalists voicing concern that a sport of elegance and beauty could degenerate into a crude form of gymnastics. Throughout it all the FIS had to tread carefully. Technical advances could not be arrested if they could be safely accommodated.

When Matti Nykanen won the Large (K90) Hill event to bring the Calgary Olympics to a spectacular close, nobody realised that it was the last time the 'parallel skis' method would be seen in Olympic competition. Regrettable as it was that the graceful classical style should disappear from all but the lower reaches of the sport, it was proved beyond all doubt by 1991 that the V-style was more efficient once the jumper had, quite literally, got the hang of it.

It was fitting that Nykanen, the supreme exponent of the old style should bring the era to a close with a flourish that was made all the more dramatic by microphones aside the track. Bent upwards by air pressure and suction, his skis hit the flat with a resounding slap which came over the amplifier system like a shockwave. His feet had touched down a micro-second before the impact, but a very heavy landing was made to look routine. Twenty-three per cent of his flight had been beyond the critical point, the largest proportion ever achieved in the days of the parallel skis.

So it was that as Nykanen plumbed the depths of the hill, the classic style went out of Olympic competition, not just with a bang, but to a great gasp of disbelief from the crowd. Neither they nor any of the old hands gathered together that day had seen anything quite like it before.

With the V-style such dangerously long jumps far beyond the critical point proved to be more easily achieved. Even such successful men as the Austrian pair of Andreas Felder and Ernst Vettori, and Jens Weissflog who joined the unified German team after years with East Germany, found themselves flying a massive twelve per cent further once they had adapted to it. It was also found that Boklov's prototype version of V-style could be considerably improved, and before long there was a marked contrast between his style and the very flat aerodynamic profile brilliantly shown off by the likes of Noriaki Kasai (Japan) and Toni Nieminen (Finland).

Up to this point it had always been the accepted norm that the average take-off speed on a Normal (K70) Hill should be about 84kph, and that on a Large (K90) Hill it should be about 91kph. Starting points on the in-runs were set accordingly, for at these speeds only the very best could go beyond the critical points, and in contrast to Alpine racing where speeds of 130kph are common, ski jumping had maintained an enviable safety record. Rather than shorten the in-runs and curtail speed for the new era of the V-style, the FIS decided that the landing slopes would have to be extended very considerably.

Baklov, now outclassed and retired, could have chuckled to himself at the huge cost of these alterations. As a result of the revolution which he started, the dimensions of the sport were upgraded as never before:

Before V-style

	Large Hill	*Normal Hill*
Hill size	K90m	K70m
Approximate take-off speed	91kph	84kph

For the new V-style age

Hill size	K120m	K90m
Approximate take-off speed	91kph	84kph

The new arrangements did much to reduce excessive distances beyond the critical point, but other problems emerged. The most successful V-jumpers were those of light body weight, and like certain species of butterflies whose outspread outline they somewhat resembled, they tended to drift off course. Gusts and side winds were liable to shift them one way or another, and on larger hills this was all the more likely to happen. The danger was greatly reduced by widening landing slopes and out-runs, and erected wind shields, but the problem of drastic weight reduction among the jumpers themselves is liable to persist.

At the FIS Congress in Melbourne in 2000, a German motion calling for a minimum body weight was defeated. For one thing such a ruling would have served to penalise the teenagers who are now part of the scene. In 1992 Nykanen's successor as Olympic champion in the new K120 event was the sixteen year-old Lahti schoolboy Toni Nieminen. In second place came Martin Hollwarth (Austria) who at seventeen was less than a year older. They were the only two to reach the critical point. The V-style was still in its infancy in 1992, and since then the best men have come to surpass their standards. The apprenticeship of a champion now takes a little longer, with the result that school-boys are no longer given time off to go from classroom to the podium with the same impunity.

In 1994 at Lillenhammer the distances cleared in the K120 event were much longer but they have since levelled off, due in part to regulations on equipment. The length of a jumper's skis for instance must not exceed 146 per cent of his height.

It is in ski flying that the greatest progress has been seen, if 'progress' it can be called. With jumpers cruising almost motionless for eight seconds over distances well in excess of 200m, ski flying attracts multi-million audiences through the main European and Japanese television channels, and revenues to match. At the same time the sport is particularly vulnerable to unfavourable weather conditions, and it is often impossible to start competitions at advertised times and dates, or to finish them within allocated time spans for the paymasters of television. In spite of these problems there is constant media demand for yet larger hills and ever greater world records.

Environmental considerations may however prevent the construction of too many of these gigantic hills which are all K185. At present there are five locations which have them: Kulm (Austria), Oberstdorf (Germany), Planica (Slovenia), Harrachov (Czech Republic) and Vikersund (Norway). Partly owned by their local communities, they have their own association, KOP. Since a disastrous World Ski Flying Championships at Kulm in 1986 when there were many accidents, KOP has become an efficient body for re-establishing responsibility, adherence to FIS rules, and restraint in the pursuit of records. It is not the policy of the FIS to encourage records, or even to keep a list of them.

Media considerations on the other hand do not exactly place the safety of the ski jumpers as their first priority, and juries in charge of these competitions can find themselves under considerable pressure. The jury is a legal requirement to ensure a safe and fair competition, and recently the FIS decided to increase their number from three to four. They are the sole authority responsible for deciding on such matters as in-run lengths, and whether or not the weather is fit for jumping to take place. They must also decide on protests, disputes and so on.

So what of the future? If ski flying is to become an Olympic sport the hills have to be available. The Americans have hosted the Winter Olympics five times, but they have only one ski flying hill at Iron Mountain, Michigan. In size this almost matches those in Europe, but whether there is sufficient interest in the US to sustain such hills is questionable. There are other parts of the world where enthusiasm for ski jumping is growing, and at the start of the third millennium it looks as if the South Koreans are destined for a place among the elite.

With over a million skiers, the Koreans have watched the progress of the Japanese over the years, and in the 1990s obtained advice from the FIS on hill construction, and top class coaching from Germany. At Muju they now have a huge centre with six jumping hills ranging from a children's starter of K8 to K120, and progress has been dramatic. In the four-man team event at the 1998 Olympics the Koreans finished a distant last in thirteenth place with only 372 points. In 2002 their team mustered 801 points to take eighth place ahead of Norway and four other countries. Keen and well organised they can only get better and better.

The upper structure at Holmenkollen with Oslo fjord in the background

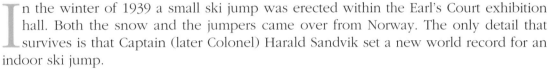

CHAPTER V
THE BRITISH AT HOME AND AWAY

Ski jumping in Britain

In the winter of 1939 a small ski jump was erected within the Earl's Court exhibition hall. Both the snow and the jumpers came over from Norway. The only detail that survives is that Captain (later Colonel) Harald Sandvik set a new world record for an indoor ski jump.

The previous record had been held by Carl Hovelsen, a Holmenkollen medallist, who made his living as the great attraction in the circus of Barnum and Bailey which toured the USA after World War I. Florid posters announced his 'perilous flights of over seventy-five feet spanning a yawning death inviting chasm'. Allowing for the hype, the distances were probably more like 60ft (18m).

World War II prevented further performances at Earls Court, and Sandvik was to distinguish himself in the Norwegian resistance as commander of the Varg (Wolf) base.

In 1904 Edward Richardson wrote that 'if the British Isles, were like Scandinavia, under snow throughout nearly half the year, we should every year be hearing of fine 100ft jumps at Hampstead Heath, as well as at Holmenkollen'. Forty-six years later, Richardson's dream virtually came true, for a 93ft (28.3m) jump was achieved at Hampstead Heath in 1950, and without any catastrophic change in climate. Richardson lived to see it for he died in 1955. Also in 1950 another group of Norwegians gave a demonstration on a slightly smaller hill in Edinburgh.

In March 1960 ski jumping came to Reddish Vale thanks to the initiative of two Norwegian students at Manchester University. Some 40ft (12.2m) of scaffolding was set above a steep embankment which made a natural landing slope. Refrigerated vans brought snow from Devil's Elbow in Scotland, and as at Hampstead Heath, jumpers were crashing into huge piles of loose hay at the bottom. Twenty-two Norwegians were joined by Tim Ashburner and Alan Crompton. The latter had been captain of the British Olympic team at Cortina in 1956, and had also become the first to cross the English Channel on water skis, having been towed to Calais and back by a speed-boat piloted by Donald Campbell. Unfortunately Crompton had to retire after the first round at Reddish with broken ribs. Ove Johnsen's jump of 106ft (32m) remained a record for fifteen months until the great show at Wembley in the summer of 1961.

Hampstead Heath 1950

Friday 24th March
Saturday 25th March
Promoters
Norges Skiforbund
Ski Club of Great Britain
Central Council for Physical Recreation

12 year old Erling Sranden jumping at Wembley, 1961. He became Norwegian National Champion in 1969 (George Konig)

Hampstead Heath, 1950

Reddish Vale, Manchester, 1960

Wembley Stadium, 1961 (George Konig)

Tim Ashburner, Tony Kennai and Alex Sykes (George Konig)

Having staged a successful ski jumping show in Denmark in 1949, the Norwegians sent 45 tons of snow and 25 jumpers, and set up the 60ft (18m) scaffold on a modest hill.

Spectators
18,000 paid the entry fee on Friday, and 52,000 at the two Saturday performances, but numbers more than doubled by gatecrashers.

Arne Hoel was the overall winner, with Reidar Andersen making the longest jump of 93ft (28·3m).

Reddish Vale 1960

Saturday 3rd March
Sunday 4th March
Promoters
Lars Eie and Erik Hoff, both students at Manchester University, to raise money for the Appeal in World Refugee Year.

Spectators
About 25,000 over two performances.

Ove Johnsen was the overall winner and made the longest jump of 106 ft.

Wembley Station 1961

Teams came from Norway, Sweden, Finland, Switzerland, France, Austria, Italy and West Germany. The structure rose to a starting point 150ft (45·7m) above football level to form a perfectly contoured K30 hill. Plastic matting was used on the in-run. The overall winner was Veikko Kankkonen (Finland) who became Olympic champion in 1964. Torgeir Brandtzag (Norway) made the longest jump of 113ft (34·5m). Thanks to the generous hospitality of Sir Charles Taylor, several illustrious names over-indulged, and provided the biggest spills. As a result the British team of Alex Sykes, Tony Kennaway and Tim Ashburner finished off the bottom. Sykes's final jump of 90ft (27·4m) indicated what might have been if some training had been possible.

The British reappear

Many years after the species was pronounced extinct, the British ski jumper was sighted again in the rarefied atmosphere of the 1988 Winter Olympics at Calgary, and the world's media attention became alerted to 'Eddie the Eagle'. At times it was made to look as if all the other jumpers were mere background support to the main attraction.

Eddie Edwards, twenty-three, a plasterer from Cheltenham, first skied while on a school trip to Italy. Nearer home there was the dry ski slope of Gloucester where he showed some aptitude for Slalom, and it was on a trip to Lake Placid for some Slalom races that he started ski jumping. The summer of 1986 was spent at Kandersteg where the Swiss National Nordic Centre very kindly gave him free use of their plastic hills.

At the time it was still relatively easy for any nation affiliated to the FIS to enter for World Cup events ski jumpers who they judged to be competent enough, and with Calgary as the target, the British Ski Federation entered Eddie for his first World Cup event at Oberstdorft on 30 December 1986. The Norwegian, Vegaard Opaas, who became World 70m Champion that winter, won with 94m. Eddie jumped 68m, and although this placed him last of the 112 competitors, it was nevertheless a remarkable achievement for one who had started ski jumping only a year before to jump 72 per cent of the winner's distance. He had undergone none of the usual apprenticeship through the lower divisions and the European Cup. Great things were expected, yet incredibly this first effort proved to be much the best of his career. In eleven more World Cup, and six European Cup appearances over the next fifteen months, as well as a World Championship and the Olympics, his form plummeted, and only revived slightly.

A year after that appearance at Oberstdorf, Eddie returned to take part in the other three of the Four Hills; Garmisch, Innsbruck and Bischofshofen where the lengths of his jumps were 52 per cent, 54 per cent and 52 per cent of the distances recorded by Matti Nykannen who won all three. As a warm-up for the Olympics which were only a few weeks away, this was horrifying, but John Leaning, the Nordic Director of the BSF had already persuaded the British Olympic Association to include him in the team. At Calgary, Eddie rallied from these low points, but could still only manage 60 per cent and 61 per cent of the lengths achieved by Nykanen who monopolised the two Olympic events in the same manner as the World Cup. What the media wanted though, and many of the fans, was an eccentric of sorts, and it apparently helped that his form was inversely proportional to the time spent talking about it.

Special mention should be made however of Eddie's very brave performances in the last rounds of the 1987 World Cup in Oslo. For the 70m event held under floodlight on the night of 20 March the weather was atrocious with snow flying everywhere. The old Midtstubakken, now demolished, had no shelter over the starting pen, and jumpers

After Eddie Edwards

ØB
Østlandets Blad – din lokalavis

I skyggen av Bredesen

Her er hoppsportens siste amatører

Norwegian newspaper's front page

awaiting their turn were completely exposed to the elements. For Eddie, with his thick glasses to keep clear as well as his goggles, it was as stiff a test of his composure as could possibly be imagined. After the take-off, he 'couldn't see a thing', but his 56m which was 66 per cent of the winner's distance earned an enormous cheer from a crowd that was soon to erupt into a state of riotous rejoicing when Vegaard Opaas's second jump of 85m confirmed him as World 70m Champion.

Two days later Eddie became only the second British ski jumper to compete at Holmenkollen. In the fifty-four years since Colin Wyatt's day the hill had doubled in size, and although the weather had improved, it was still dreary, with the upper structure often hidden in cloud. The crowd of 50,000 was well below capacity, most people preferring to watch on television. Andreas Felder (Austria) won with 104m and 105m.

Eddie cleared 67m (64 per cent), and as at Midtstubakken finished just ahead of the only other Lowlander, Gerrit Konijnenberg (Holland).

Konijnenberg, the original flying Dutchman, made enormous progress over the next three years, but then retired to develop ski jumping among his countrymen. Holland may be flat, but across the border in the Sauerland hills of Germany there are the plastic ski jump centres of Meinerzhagen, Willingen and Winterberg with jumps of all sizes.

When Eddie returned to the Holmenkollen in 1988, he could only jump 60m, but others were beginning to appear, and with the prospect of forming a British team, generous sponsorship was provided by Barbour Index, the building information specialists.

Alan Jones and James Lambert had been living and working in Garmisch for a few years. Jones, a refrigeration mechanic, competed at weekends in regional competitions, and first met Eddie Edwards at a European Cup event at St Moritz in December 1987 when he finished well behind him.

James Lambert chucked in a job in a mental institution in Rochdale and took a one-way ticket to Munich. Speaking no German, and with neither money nor qualifications, he nevertheless found a job as a mountain guide at a large US servicemen's recreation centre, and was soon abseiling his charges over the abyss with all the impunity of a building labourer letting down a waste bucket from the upper scaffolding. Such apparently are the opportunities within the EC, that a winter job as a ski instructor followed, and his attraction to ski jumping.

The best of a large number of beginners and occasional jumpers who came to training camps after Eddie's appearance at Calgary was Ben Freeth. For him as well as for Lambert and Jones, the Barbour Index sponsorship came at just the right time. Trainers were found in Franz Kurz, a former trainer of the German national team, and Geir Hammer in Norway.

With the 'V-style' revolution, and the increases in the sizes of hills used for major competitions, both the FIS and the IOC introduced stiff qualifications for entry licences into the top level which effectively consigned the British, among others, to the ranks. The European Cup was still open, but a more realistic option which the FIS encouraged was to include ski jumping in the FIS Lowlanders Championships which attracts a very large and enthusiastic entry every year to the various cross country races for seniors and juniors of both sexes.

The first Lowlanders Ski Jumping Championships were held in 1992 on the 50m hill at Scheidegg in Allgau in Baden Wurtemberg. The field consisted of three British, five Dutch and a Ugandan. Notable absentees, because of distance, were the Hungarians whose ski jumpers are of much the same standard, but it was greatly to the credit of all nine that they were so keen to compete in the poor conditions. It was early March and the landing slope resembled a sodden strip of paper towel hanging from its canister. Alan Jones who jumped 43m and 41m won, with Ben Freeth second. They were the only ones to stand on both rounds. Peter van Hal had the longest jump of 48m and also the biggest fall. Dunstan Odeke of Uganda hurt himself, but when he later settled in Oslo, as did Lambert and Jones he regularly jumped 50m and became undisputed Champion of all Africa.

To ensure better conditions in 1993 it was decided to hold the event on 3 September on the 70m plastic hill at Meinerzhagen, 50km east of Cologne. This time Peter van Hal won it for Holland with two jumps of 64m. Lambert and Freeth were second and third. Eddie Edwards did not compete in either of these two Lowlanders which unfortunately proved to be the first and the last. It was possible to see how he compared with Lambert however when both were entered for a European Cup event at St Aegyd am Neuwald in Austria on 29 December 1992. Lambert came sixty-second out of sixty-seven with a jump of 54m (75 per cent of the winner's distance) which placed him ahead of all three Hungarians, a Russian, and Eddie who was last with 46m.

In consolation for the British being unable to qualify for the Lillehammer Olympics of 1994, the Norwegians very kindly invited Lambert, Freeth and Jones to forerun the

The forward position

Norwegian National Championships on the Holmenkollen in February 1994. It was a great honour, for the task has to be given to reliable men, and can be daunting if new tram-lines have to be laid, straight and true, after a snowfall. The Holmenkollen had once again been slightly enlarged since Eddie appeared there a few years before, but no further snow had fallen since the training rounds of the day before. Lambert led the way with 80m; Freeth followed with 75m and Jones with 72m. The following morning the three were accorded as much publicity in the Norwegian newspapers as the top performers. The winner jumped 111m which was 28 per cent more than Lambert's effort which was arguably a British record for he had started from the same point as the competitors, even if he was not in the actual competition itself.

In jumping over 70m, the trio joined Eddie Edwards as members of the exclusive Ski Club for the over 70s, to which are also admitted the growing number of British langlaufers who have successfully completed Ski Marathons of 70km or more. With Ben Freeth and Alan Jones opting to retire, it was decided to end the sponsorship of Barbour Index whose continued support had made this appearance on the most famous of all hills possible. The British ski jumping team was therefore put into suspension until another day.

Matti Nykanen in the starting gate

CHAPTER VI
TECHNICAL

The design of jumping hills

The safety of ski jumping is incorporated in the design of the hill. Unless the profiles of a ski jump satisfy the requirements of the FIS, it cannot be authorised for competition. The FIS Certificate amounts to a licence for use, and organising committees would be unable to get insurance cover without it.

The FIS, if satisfied after carrying out their own independent measurements, especially on newly constructed hills, will award a Certificate which will generally be valid for a few years. Before they renew it at the end of that period, they may want to check some of the dimensions again. Landing slopes can get furrowed with use, and soil consolidation on new hills can be a problem. In 1991 the landing slope of the new K104 hill at Stams in Austria gave way in a landslide and had to be rebuilt. Ski jumps therefore need to have curves which are neither too flat nor over-inflated.

Size

Jumping hills are known by their 'K' size. This is the distance from the edge of the take-off to the point K (critical point) which marks the bottom of the steepest section of the landing slope, and which is shown as W (weite or length).

Vertical height

The difference in height between the topmost starting point and the bottom of a ski jump is seldom shown on the charts. The main reason for this is because the amount of in-run used in competition is always less than what is available. In order to curtail speeds the start bar may be set across any one of a number of entry steps (es) at the top of the in-run.

Typically however the total height of a small hill is one-third more than its figure for K (or W). Thus for a K30 hill it would be 40m. As the K size increases, this proportion decreases to less than a quarter. On a typical K90 hill the highest starting point would be 110m.

The landing slope

The flight paths of V-style jumpers tend to be flatter and longer than they used to be. In the days of the parallel skis the arc of the flight path was more pronounced and it was very dangerous if a jumper reached a point deep in the r2 curve where the angle of the slope might be only 30°. Because of their lower trajectories the V-style jumpers come in to land at a finer angle, and a slope of 30° does not pose a problem.

In one respect therefore the jumpers had made the sport safer for themselves, but problems arose on the steepest section between P and K where the angle used to be about 37°. Here the angle at landing is at its narrowest, and it proved to be too fine for V-stylists who had got into trouble in their flight and were landing off balance. To stand a chance of righting themselves they needed a bit more contact with the slope in the moment of touch-down.

Significant alterations to the lower profile of the landing slope were necessary in order to make it less steep. In 1997 the FIS came up with the new formula which was to extend this part of the hill outwards, to establish a new point L below K, and whereas the r2 curve used to start from K; it was now to begin from L.

P and K were formerly connected by a straight section, and still are on small hills where these alterations have not had to be carried out. Now, P, K and L are connected by a slight curve. As a result the angle of the slope at K has been made slightly less steep than before.

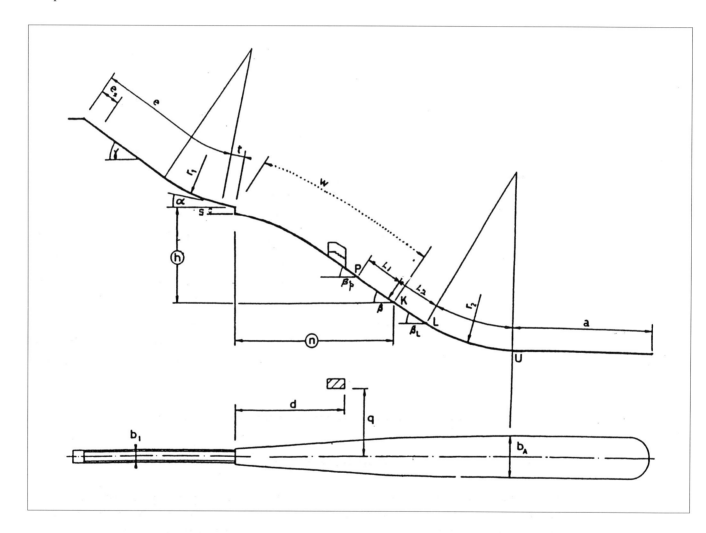

	Swiss Nordic Centre Kandersteg		Park City, Utah		Vikersund
	K30	K60	K90	K120	K185
e	42m	74m	83m	98m	103.34m
es	10·74m	17m	20m	25m	24·20m
t	4·40m	5·20m	6·30m	6·70m	7
४	32°	27·5°	35°	35°	40°
∝	7°	10°	10°	10·5°	11°
r1	39-50m	70-125m	82m	93m	105-157m
h	13·60m	28·43m	43·16m	59·52m	95·59m
n	25m	52·47m	78·47m	103·51m	157·62m
s	·83m	2·01m	2·30m	3m	3·65m
l1			11·74m	18·67m	30·81m
l2			10m	13·90m	21·90m
a	60m	90m	90m	90m	90m
ß_			37.50°	38°	38°
ß			35·00°	35°	35°
ßL			32·87°	32·77°	32·86°
r1			269m	356m	588m
r2	48m	95-132m	104m	105m	115m
P	24m	45m	78·26m	101·33m	154m
K (W)	30m	60m	90m	120m	185m
L			100m	133·90m	207m
b1	2·50m	2·50m	2·50m	2·50m	3·50m
ba	9m	13m	19·50m	26·50m	41m
d			56m	84·30m	78·63m
q			25·50m	51·50m	36·40m

The scoring system

In competition ski jumpers are marked for distance and style. A panel of five judges each award style points up to a maximum of twenty. The highest and lowest of these five markings are then eliminated, and the totals of the other three are added up. There are therefore a maximum of sixty points available for style.

For distance there is no maximum exactly, but the critical point (K) serves as par, and is worth sixty points whatever is the size of the hill. It takes a good jumper to reach it, just as it takes a golfer of comparative ability to par the course. The FIS scale which decides how many extra points he gains for exceeding the K point, or loses for falling short, takes into account the size of the hill.

The V-style caused a re-think on these values, and by 1998 they were revised downwards. Both the old values and the new are shown here because they explain how it was that Espen Bredesen won the 1994 Olympic K90 event with a record total of 282·0 points, and why later winners have achieved rather less.

Size of hill		Previous value of 1·0m	New value of 1·0m
K =	20 to 24m	4.8	3.2
	25 to 29m	4·4	3·0
	30 to 34m	4·0	2·8
	35 to 39m	3·6	2·6
	40 to 49m	3·2	2·4
	50 to 59m	2·8	2·2
	60 to 69m	2·4	2·0
	70 to 79m	2·2	1·3
	80 to 99m	2·0	1·6
	100 to 120m	1·8	1·4
	145 to 185m	1·2	1·0

On page 101 are the results of that 1994 Olympic Normal Hill event at Lillehammer. There were fifty-eight starters, and in order to gain a clear picture of the workings of the points system, the scores for the top seven are shown, and also the scores for those who finished twenty-fifth, fortieth and fifty-sixth.

For a hill with a critical point (K) of 90m, the table shows that the value of each 1·0m beyond the K point, or short of it used to be 2 points.

Bredesen's first jump was 10.5m beyond K. Thus he gained an extra 21 points (10·5 x 2) over the par of 60, for 81 points. His superb style won full 20s from three judges, and 19·5s from the other two. The highest and lowest have to be eliminated, which in this case means one of each of these scores, to leave him with 20·0 + 20·0 + 19·5 for a total of 59·5. This is a score that is very rarely achieved, and only 0·5 point off the maximum possible. Added to his 81 for distance, this gave him 140·5 for the jump. Distance accounted for 60 per cent of his final total of 282·0 points.

Only 2·5 points separated third place from seventh. Kasai with the best style points over two rounds, held on to fifth place ahead of men with greater distances.

Less than half way down the finishing list we see that distance and style points each account for 50 per cent of the 213·0 points gained by Freiholz who came twenty-fifth. Freiholz and his fellow Swiss, Trunz (fortieth), both had disastrous second jumps. Many others recorded large differences in distances over two jumps, an indication that wind could have presented problems, but the figures tell us that the best were coping rather better than the rest.

Trunz's second jump of 68·5m was 21·5m short of K, resulting in the loss of 43 points off the par 60, for a wretched 17. Over two jumps his distance points accounted for 42 per cent of his total, and this proportion was to rapidly diminish further towards the tail. Grybovich, fifty-sixth, had a second jump of 59·0m. At 31·0m short of K, it cost him 62 points. As par is 60, it meant a deficit of −2 which had to be subtracted from style points. As it was, his style points held up pretty well, and accounted for 94 per cent of his overall total. Eddie Edwards had been outperformed!

Scores in the 1994 Normal (K90) Hill event at Lillehammer

	Length	Pts	A	B	C	D	E		Total
1. Espen Bredesen	100·5m	81	20·0	19·5	20·0	20·0	19·5	140·5	
(Norway)	104·0	88	17·5	18·0	18·0	17·0	18·0	141·5	282·0
2. Lasse Ottesen	102·5	85	17·5	17·0	17·5	17·5	17·0	137·5	
(Norway)	98·0	76	19·0	18·0	18·0	18·5	18·0	130·5	268·0
3. Dieter Thoma	98·5	77	16·0	17·0	17·5	15·5	17·0	127·0	
(Germany)	102·5	85	15·5	16·5	16·5	15·5	16·5	133·5	260·5
4. Jens Weissflog	98·0	76	18·5	19·0	18·5	18·5	19·0	132·0	
(Germany)	96·5	73	17·5	18·0	18·5	18·5	18·5	128·0	260·0
5. Noriaki Kasai	98·0	76	19·5	20·0	19·0	19·5	19·5	134·5	
(Japan)	93·0	66	20·0	19·5	19·5	19·0	19·5	124·5	259·.0
6. Jani Soininen	95·0	70	18·5	19·0	18·5	18·0	18·0	122·5	
(Finland)	100·5	81	17·5	18·0	17·5	17·0	17·5	136·0	258·5
7. Andreas	98·0	76	19·5	19·0	19·0	19·5	19·0	133·5	
Goldberger (Austria)	93·5	67	19·0	19·5	19·5	18·5	19·0	124·5	258·0
25 Sylvain	94·0	68	18·5	18·0	18·0	17·5	18·5	132·5	
Freiholz	79·5	39	14·0	13·0	14·0	15·0	13·5	80·5	
(Switzerland)									213·0
40. Martin Trunz	88·5	57	18·5	18·0	18·5	18·5	18·0	112·0	
(Switzerland)	68·5	17	16·0	15·0	15·5	14·5	15·5	63·0	175·0
56. Vasyl Grybovich	64·0	8	16·5	16·5	16·5	15·5	57·5		
(Ukraine)	59·0	-2	16·0	15·5	15·5	15·0	15·5	44·5	
									102·0

Olympic records

1924 Chamonix

		FIRST JUMP (M)	SECOND JUMP (M)	TOTAL PTS.
1. Jacob Tullin Thams	NOR	49·0	49·0	18·960
2. Narve Bonna	NOR	47·5	49·0	18·689
3. Anders Haugen	USA	49·0	50·0	17·916
4. Thorleif Haug	NOR	44·0	44·5	17·821
5. Einar Landvik	NOR	42·0	44·5	17·521
6. Axel Nilsson	SWE	42·5	44·0	17·146
7. Menotti Jacobsen	SWE	43·0	42·0	17·083
8. Alexander Girarbille	SWI	40·5	41·5	16·794

1928 St Moritz

		FIRST JUMP (M)	SECOND JUMP (M)	TOTAL PTS.
1. Alf Anderson	NOR	60·0	64·0	19·208
2. Sigmund Ruud	NOR	57·5	62·5	18·542
3. Rudolf Purkert	CZE	57·0	59·5	17·937
4. Axel Nilsson	SWE	53·5	60·0	16·937
5. Sven Lundgren	SWE	48·0	59·0	16·708
6. Rolf Monsen	USA	53·0	59·5	16·687
7. Sepp Muhlbauer	SWI	52·0	58·0	16·541
8. Ernst Feuz	SWI	52·5	58·5	16·458

1932 Lake Placid

		FIRST JUMP (M)	SECOND JUMP (M)	TOTAL PTS.
1. Birger Ruud	NOR	66·5	69·0	228·1
2. Hans Beck	NOR	71·5	63·5	227·0
3. Kaare Wahlberg	NOR	65·5	64·0	218·9
5. Caspar Oimen	USA	63·0	67·5	216·7
6. Fritz Kaufmann	SWI	63·5	65·5	215·8
7. Sigmund Ruud	NOR	63·0	62·5	215·1
8. Goro Adachi	JPN	60·0	66·0	210·7

1936 Garmisch-Partenkirchen

		FIRST JUMP (M)	SECOND JUMP (M)	TOTAL PTS.
1. Birger Rudd	NOR	75·0	74·5	232·0
2. Sven Eriksson	SWE	76·0	76·0	230·5
3. Reidar Andersen	NOR	74·0	75·0	228·9
4. Kaare Wahlberg	NOR	73·5	72·0	227·0
5. Stanislaw Marusarz	POL	73·0	75·5	221·6
6. Lauri Valonen	FIN	73·5	67·0	219·4
7. Masaji Iguro	JPN	74·5	72·5	218·2
8. Arnold Kongsgaard	NOR	74·5	72·2	217·7

1948 St Moritz

		FIRST JUMP (M)	SECOND JUMP (M)	TOTAL PTS.
1. Petter Hugsted	NOR	65·0	70·0	228·1
2. Birger Rudd	NOR	64·0	67·0	226·6
3. Thorleif Schjelderup	NOR	64·0	67·0	225·1
4. Matti Pietikainen	FIN	69·5	69·0	224·6
5. Gordon Wren	USA	68·0	68·5	222·8
6. Leo Laakso	FIN	66·0	69·5	221·7
7. Asbjorn Ruud	NOR	58·0	67·5	220·2
8. Aatto Pietikainen	FIN	69·0	68·0	215·4

In what was only the fifth Winter Olympics, the small silver mining town of Kongsberg (pop: 5,000) in the province of Buskerud, rejoiced in its third consecutive gold medal in the ski jumping event when Peter Hugsted became the latest local boy to become champion, in the Fohn at St Moritz. Furthermore, Birger Rudd's second place also raised the local tally of silver medals to three. His brother Sigmund came second in 1924, as did Hans Beck in 1932.

1952 Oslo

		FIRST JUMP (M)	SECOND JUMP (M)	TOTAL PTS.
1. Arnfinn Bergmann	NOR	67·5	68·0	226·0
2. Torbjorn Falkanger	NOR	68·0	64·0	221·5
3. Karl Holmström	SWE	67·0	65·5	219·5
4. Toni Brutscher	GER	66·5	62·5	216·5
4. Halvor Naes	NOR	63·5	64·5	216·5
6. Arne Hoel	NOR	66·5	63·5	215·5
7. Antti Hyvarinen	FIN	66·5	61·5	213·5
8. Sepp Weiler	GER	67·0	63·0	213·0

The contest at Holmenkollen was watched by approximately 120,000 people, the largest ever attendance at an Olympic event. Still celebrating a string of stunning victories six days earlier, when Norwegians won the 1500m skating event, the 18km cross country race and the Nordic Combination, they came in confident expectation of more. In spite of the pressure, Falkanger and Bergmann led on the first round. Bergmann chose what proved to be the slightly faster of two in-run tracks for the second round, and won comfortably.

1956 Cortina

		FIRST JUMP (M)	SECOND JUMP (M)	TOTAL PTS
1. Antti Hyvarinen	FIN	81·0	84·0	227·0
2. Aulis Kallakorpi	FIN	83·5	80·5	225·0
3. Harry Glass	GDR	83·5	80·5	224·5
4. Max Bolkart	GER	80·0	81·5	222·5
5. Sven Pettersson	SWE	81·0	81·5	220·0
6. Andreas Dascher	SWI	82·0	82·0	219·5
7. Eino Kirjonen	FIN	78·0	81·0	219·0
8. Werner Lesser	GDR	77·5	77·5	210·0

Showing superb aerodynamic style with arms pressed alongside their bodies, Hyvarinen and Kallakorpi ended Norwegian domination of Olympic ski jumping.

1960 Squaw Valley

		FIRST JUMP (M)	SECOND JUMP (M)	TOTAL PTS.
1. Helmut Recknagel	GDR	93·5	84·5	227·2

		FIRST JUMP	SECOND JUMP	TOTAL
2. Nilo Halonen	FIN	92·5	83·5	222·6
3. Otto Leodolter	AUT	88·5	83·5	219.4
4. Nikolai Kamensky	SPV/RUS	90·5	79·0	216·9
5. Thorbjorn Yggeseth	NOR	88·5	82·5	216·1
6. Max Bolkart	GER	87·5	81·0	212·6
7. Ansten Samuelstuen	USA	90·0	79·0	211·5
8. Juhani Karkinen	FIN	87·5	82·0	211·4

For weeks afterwards, television networks and cinemas around the world showed slow motion sequences of Recknagel's effortless flights with his arms stretched out in front. Such was his perfection that no one could have foreseen that it was to be the last time a major title would be won with this method, although Arne Larsen (Norway) used it on his way to winning the Nordic Combination at the World Championships of 1962 at Zakopane.

1964 Innsbruck-Seefeld

		FIRST JUMP (M)	SECOND JUMP (M)	TOTAL PTS.
1. Veikko Kankkonen	FIN	80·0	79·0	229·9
2. Toralf Engan	NOR	79·0	79·0	226·3
3. Torgeir Brandtzaeg	NOR	79·0	78·0	222·9
4. Josef Matous	CZE	80·5	77·0	218·2
5. Dieter Neuendorf	GDR	78·5	77·0	214·7
6. Helmut Recknagel	GDR	77·0	75·5	210·4
7. Kurt Elima	SWE	76·0	75·0	208·9
8. Hans Olav Sörensen	NOR	76·0	74·5	208·6

1964 Innsbruck

		FIRST JUMP (M)	SECOND JUMP (M)	TOTAL PTS.
1. Toralf Engan	NOR	93·5	90·5	230·7
2. Veikko Kankkonen	FIN	95·5	90·5	228·9
3. Torgeir Brandtzaeg	NOR	92·0	90·0	227·2
4. Dieter Bokeloh	GDR	92·0	83·5	214·6
5. Kjell Sjöberg	SWE	90·0	85·0	214·4
6. Aleksandr Ivannikov	SOV/RUS	90·0	83·5	213·3
7. Helmut Recknagel	GDR	89·0	86·5	212·8
8. Dieter Neuendorf	GDR	92·5	84·5	212·6

A second ski jumping competition was added in 1964 to provide greater opportunity to win medals in a sport where a sudden gust of wind or a split second mistake can result in defeat. Veikko Kankkonen made such a mistake on his first jump in what was now the Normal Hill event. Fortunately for him the 1964 competition was the only one in which each man had three jumps, with the best two to count, and he was able to recover and win. As it turned out, the same three men took the medals in both events, with Engan winning on the Large Hill on the strength of his peerless style.

1968 Grenoble-Autrans

		FIRST JUMP (M)	SECOND JUMP (M)	TOTAL PTS.
1. Jiri Raska	CZE	79·0	72·5	216·5
2. Reinhold Bachler	AUT	77·5	76·0	214·2
3. Baldur Preiml	AUT	80·0	72·5	212·6
4. Björn Wirkola	NOR	76·5	72·5	212·0
5. Topi Mattila	FIN	78·0	72·5	211·9
6. Anatoly Zheglanov	SOV/RUS	79·5	74·5	211·5
7. Dieter Neuendorf	GDR	76·5	73·0	211·3
8. Vladimir Belousov	SOV/RUS	73·5	73·0	207·5

1968 Grenoble-St Nizier

		FIRST JUMP (M)	SECOND JUMP (M)	TOTAL PTS.
1. Vladimir Belousov	SOV/RUS	101·5	98·5	231·3
2. Jiri Raska	CZE	101·0	98·0	229·4
3. Lars Grini	NOR	99·0	93·5	214·3
4. Manfred Queck	GDR	96·5	98·5	212·8
5. Bent Tomtum	NOR	98·5	95·0	212·2
6. Reinhold Bachler	AUT	98·5	95·0	210·7
7. Wolfgang Stöhr	GDR	96·5	92·5	205·9
8. Anatoly Zheglanov	SOV/RUS	99·0	92·0	205·7

With a gold and silver for his efforts at Grenoble, Jiri Raska, a bear of a man from Czechoslovakia became his country's most successful ski jumper.

1972 Sapporo-Miyanomori

		FIRST JUMP (M)	SECOND JUMP (M)	TOTAL PTS.
1. Yaukio Kasaya	JPN	84·0	79·0	244·2
2. Akitsugu Konno	JPN	82·5	79·0	234·8
3. Seiji Aochi	JPN	83·5	77·5	229·5
4. Ingolf Mork	NOR	78·0	78·0	225·5
5. Jiri Raska	CZE	78·5	78·0	224·8
6. Wojciech Fortuna	POL	82·0	76·5	222·0
7. Karel Kodejska	CZE	80·0	75·5	220·2
7. Gari Napalkov	SOV/RUS	79·5	76·0	220·2

1972 Sapporo-Okurayama

		FIRST JUMP (M)	SECOND JUMP (M)	TOTAL PTS.
1. Wojciech Fortuna	POL	111·0	87·5	219·9
2. Walter Steiner	SWI	94·0	103·0	219·8
3. Rainer Schmidt	GDR	98·5	101·0	219·3

4. Tauno Kayhko	FIN	95·0	100·5	219·2
5. Manfred Wolf	GDR	107·0	89·5	215·1
6. Gari Napalkov	SOV/RUS	99·5	92·0	210·1
7. Yukio Kasaya	JPN	106·0	85·0	209·4
8. Danilo Pudgar	YUG/SLO	97·5	97·5	206·0

An account of the Japanese clean-sweep of the medals on the Normal Hill appears on page 82. On the Large Hill at Okurayama five days later the winds posed problems, especially during the later stages of the competition. Going last, the first round leaders all landed well short of the first efforts, but such was Fortuna's massive early lead that in spite of a second jump that was 23·5m shorter, he was able to win the gold medal by the narrowest possible margin. The first four were separated by less than a single point.

1976 Innsbruck-Seefeld

		FIRST JUMP M)	SECOND JUMP (M)	TOTAL PTS.
1. Hans-George Aschenbach	GDR	84·5	82·0	252·0
2. Jochen Danneberg	GDR	83·5	82·5	246·2
3. Karl Schnabl	AUT	82·5	81·5	242·0
4. Jaroslav Balcar	CZE	81·0	81·5	239·6
5. Ernst von Gruningen	SWI	80·5	80·5	238·7
6. Reinhold Bachler	AUT	80·5	80·5	237·2
7. Anton Innauer	AUT	80·5	81·5	233·5
7. Rudolf Wanner	AUT	79·5	79·5	233·5

1976 Innsbruck

		FIRST JUMP (M)	SECOND JUMP (M)	TOTAL PTS.
1. Karl Schnabl	AUT	97·5	97·0	234·8
2. Anton Innauer	AUT	102·5	91·0	232·9
3. Henry Glass	GDR	91·0	97·0	221·7
4. Jochen Danneberg	GDR	102·0	89·5	221·6
5. Reinhold Bachler	AUT	95·0	91·0	217·4
6. Hans Wallner	AUT	93·5	92·5	216·9
7. Bernd Eckstein	GDR	94·0	91·5	216·2
8. Hans-Georg Aschenbach	GDR	92·5	89·0	212·1

As usual, questions were raised about the East German triumph at Seefeld. Aschenbach later admitted to having taken anabolic steroids for eight years, and described how, in the hour of his victory, he felt pulverised with anxiety as he went along to doping control and awaited the results. He got away with it, but wondered whether it was worth it. As at Sapporo, the host city celebrated wildly when Schnabl and the seventeen-year-old Innauer came first and second on the Berg Isel in what was mainly a contest between Austria and East Germany.

1980 Lake Placid

		FIRST JUMP (M)	SECOND JUMP (M)	TOTAL PTS.
1. Anton Innauer	AUT	89·0	90·0	266·3
2. Manfred Deckert	GDR	85·0	88·0	249·2
2. Hirokazu Yagi	JPN	87·0	83·5	249·2
4. Masahiro Akimoto	JPN	83·5	87·5	248·5
5. Pentti Kokkonen	FIN	86·0	83·5	247·6
6. Hubert Neuper	AUT	82·5	88·5	245·5
7. Alfred Groyer	AUT	85·5	83·5	245·3
8. Jouko Tormanen	FIN	83·0	85·5	243·5

1980 Lake Placid

		FIRST JUMP (M)	SECOND JUMP (M)	TOTAL PTS.
1. Jouko Tormanen	FIN	114·5	117·0	271·0
2. Hubert Neuper	AUT	113·0	114·5	262·4
3. Jiri Puikkonen	FIN	110·5	109·5	248·5
4. Anton Innauer	AUT	110·0	107·0	245·7
5. Armin Kogler	AUT	110·0	108·0	245·6
6. Roger Rudd	NOR	110·0	109·0	243·0
7. Hansjorg Sumi	SWI	117·0	110·0	242·7
8. James Denney	USA	109·0	104·0	239·1

Now twenty-one, Toni Innauer was a ski jumper of extraordinary elegance, and won the Normal Hill easily. Hansjorg Sumi from Gstaad produced a spectacular first jump on the Large Hill, but did not land easily and lost vital points.

1984 Sarajevo

		FIRST JUMP (M)	SECOND JUMP (M)	TOTAL PTS.
1. Jens Weissflog	GDR	90·0	87·0	215·2
2. Matti Nykanen	FIN	91·0	84·0	214·0
3. Jari Puikkonen	FIN	81·5	91·5	212·8
4. Stefan Stannarius	GDR	84·0	89·5	211·1
5. Rolf Åge Berg	NOR	86·0	86·5	208·5
6. Andreas Felder	AUT	84·0	87·0	205·6
7. Piotr Fijas	POL	87·0	88·0	204·5
8. Vegard Opaas	NOR	86·0	87·0	203·8

1984 Sarajevo

		FIRST JUMP (M)	SECOND JUMP (M)	TOTAL PTS.
1. Matti Nykanen	FIN	116·0	111·0	231·2
2. Jens Weissflog	GDR	107·0	107·5	213·7

		FIRST JUMP (M)	SECOND JUMP (M)	TOTAL PTS.
3. Pavel Ploc	CZE	103·5	109·0	202·9
4. Jeffrey Hastings	USA	102·5	107·0	201·2
5. Jari Puikkonen	FIN	103·5	102·0	196·6
6. Armin Kogler	AUT	106·0	99·5	195·6
7. Andreas Bauer	GER	105·0	100·5	194·6
8. Vladimir Podzimek	CZE	98·5	108·0	194·5

Nykanen and the nineteen-year-old Weissflog were both favourites to win the two events at Sarajevo. Nykanen won the Large Hill by a record margin of 17·5 points.

1988 Calgary

		FIRST JUMP (M)	SECOND JUMP (M)	TOTAL PTS.
1. Matti Nykanen	FIN	89·5	89·5	229·1
2. Pavel Ploc	CZE	84·5	87·0	212·1
3. Jiri Malec	CZE	88·0	85·5	211·8
4. Miran Tepes	YUG	84·0	83·5	211·2
5. Jiri Parma	CZE	83·5	82·5	203·8
6. Heinz Kuttin	AUT	87·0	80·5	199·7
7. Jiri Puikkonen	FIN	84·0	80·0	199·1
8. Staffan Tallberg	SWE	83·0	81·0	198·1

1988 Calgary

		FIRST JUMP (M)	SECOND JUMP (M)	TOTAL PTS.
1. Matti Nykanen	FIN	118·5	107·0	224·0
2. Erik Johnsen	NOR	114·5	102·0	207·9
3. Matjaz Debelak	YUG/SLO	113·0	108·0	207·7
4. Thomas Klauser	GER	114·5	102·5	205·1
5. Pavel Ploc	CZE	114·5	102·5	204·1
6. Andreas Felder	AUT	113·5	103·0	203·9
7. Horst Bulau	CAN	112·5	99·5	197·6
8. Staffan Tallberg	SWE	110·0	102·0	196·6

The Large Hill event was delayed four times because of dangerous winds, but rivals' hopes that the delays would finally unsettle the notoriously ill-tempered Nykanen were dashed. After two more wins at Calgary by equal enormous margins, Nykanen became arguably the greatest ski jumper who ever lived, and there was still another gold to come when he helped Finland win the team event which was held for the first time. From five Olympic competitions he finished with four gold medals and a silver, all of which he later sold.

1992 Albertville-Courcheval

		FIRST JUMP (M)	SECOND JUMP (M)	TOTAL PTS.
1. Ernst Vettori	AUT	88·0	87·5	222·8

		FIRST JUMP (M)	SECOND JUMP (M)	TOTAL PTS.
2. Martin Hollwarth	AUT	90·5	83·0	218·1
3. Toni Nieminen	FIN	88·0	84·5	217·0
4. Heinz Kuttin	AUT	85·5	86·0	214·4
5. Mika Laitinen	FIN	85·5	85·5	213·6
6. Andreas Felder	AUT	87·0	83·0	213·5
7. Heiko Hunger	GER	87·0	84·0	211·6
8. Didier Mollard	FRA	84·5	85·0	209·7

1992 Albertville-Courcheval

		FIRST JUMP (M)	SECOND JUMP (M)	TOTAL PTS.
1. Toni Nieminen	FIN	122·0	123·0	239·5
2. Martin Hollwarth	AUT	120·5	116·5	227·3
3. Heinz Kuttin	AUT	117·5	112·0	214·8
4. Masahiko Harada	JPN	113·5	116·0	211·3
5. Jiri Parma	CZE	111·5	108·5	198·0
6. Steeve Delaup	FRA	106·0	105·5	185·6
7. Ivan Lunardi	ITA	110·5	102·5	185·2
8. Franci Petek	SLO	107·0	99·5	177·1

With a breath-taking display of the V-style technique, the sixteen-year-old Toni Nieminen became the youngest male to win a Winter Olympics gold medal in the individual event. Martin Hollwarth, second in both events, was seventeen. For neither of these unaffected young lads was life quite the same again, and neither made it to Lillehammer two years later. From the moment he flew back to Helsinki airport, Nieminen was the idol of every teenage girl in Finland. His sponsors Toyota presented him with a top of the range sports car, and although under age, the authorities gave him a driving licence.

1994 Lillehammer

		FIRST JUMP (M)	SECOND JUMP (M)	TOTAL PTS.
1. Espen Bredesen	NOR	100·5	105·0	282·0
2. Lasse Ottesen	NOR	102·5	98·0	268·0
3. Dieter Thoma	GER	98·5	102·5	260·5
4. Jens Weissflog	GER	98·0	96·5	260·0
5. Noriaki Kasai	JPN	98·0	93·0	259·0
6. Jani Markus Soininen	FIN	95·0	100·5	258·5
7. Andreas Goldberger	AUT	98·0	93·5	258·0
8. Jinya Nishikata	JPN	99·0	94·0	253·0

1994 Lillehammer

		FIRST JUMP (M)	SECOND JUMP (M)	TOTAL PTS.
1. Jens Weissflog	GER	129·5	133·0	274·5
2. Espen Bredesen	NOR	135·5	122·0	266·5

		FIRST JUMP (M)	SECOND JUMP (M)	TOTAL PTS.
3. Andreas Goldberger	AUT	128·5	121·5	255·0
4. Takanobu Okabe	JPN	117·0	128·0	243·5
5. Jani Markus Soininen	FIN	117·0	122·5	231·1
6. Lasse Ottesen	NOR	117·0	120·0	226·0
7. Jaroslav Sakala	CZE	117·0	115·5	222·0
8. Jinya Nishikata	JPN	123·5	110·5	218·3

In 1992 Espen Bredesen finished last in the Normal Hill event, and fifty-seventh out of fifty-nine on the Large Hill. He was however by far the best of the Norwegians in the Team event, but this did not prevent him from being ridiculed by Norwegian sportswriters who gave him the name of 'Espen the Eagle', a successor of 'Eddie the Eagle' Edwards who had come last at Calgary. 'I had more patience than they had jokes' he said of all the hurtful comment, when he became World Champion at Falun in Sweden in 1993. At Lillehammer before a wildly excited home crowd, his two jumps on the Normal Hill produced an Olympic record of 282 points.

Jens Weissflog's victory on the Large Hill gave him a special place in ski jumping history. It came twelve years after his first at Sarajevo in 1984. In the years between, he had to overcome injuries and difficulties adjusting to the new V-style, and his form was unpredictable, but he was still at the top when he retired two years later.

1998 Nagano
K90 Individual

		FIRST JUMP (M)	SECOND JUMP (M)	TOTAL PTS.
1. Jani Soininen	FIN	90·0	89·0	234·5
2. Kazuyoshi Funaki	JAP	87·5	90·5	233·5
3. Andreas Widholzl	AUT	88·0	90·5	232·5
4. Janne Ahonen	FIN	86·5	91·5	231·1
5. Masahiko Harada	JAP	91·5	84·5	228·5
6. Primoz Peterka	SLO	87·0	89·0	223·0
7. Noriaki Kasai	JAP	87·5	89·0	223·0
8. Kristian Brenden	NOR	87·5	84·0	215·5

K120 Individual

		FIRST JUMP (M)	SECOND JUMP (M)	TOTAL PTS.
1. Kazuyoshi Funaki	JAP	126·0	132·5	272·3
2. Jani Soininen	FIN	129·5	126·5	260·8
3. Masahiko Harada	JAP	120·0	136·0	258·3
4. Andreas Widholzl	AUT	131·0	120·5	258·2
5. Primoz Peterka	SLO	119·0	130·5	251·1
6. Takanobu Okabe	JAP	130·0	119·5	250·1
7. Reinhard Schwarzenberger	AUT	115·5	131·0	244·2
8. Michal Dolezal	CZE	116·0	130·5	243·2

Once again the Japanese enjoyed success on home ground as they had at Sapporo in 1972. They also won the team event.

2002 Salt Lake City

K90 Individual

		FIRST JUMP (M)	SECOND JUMP (M)	TOTAL PTS.
1. Simon Ammann	SWI	98·5	99·0	269·0
2. Sven Hannawald	GER	97·5	99·5	267·5
3. Adam Malysz	POL	97·0	99·0	263·0
4. Janne Ahonen	FIN	96·0	99·5	261·5
5. Veli-Matti Lindstroem	FIN	95·5	95·5	253·0
6. Matti Hautamaeki	FIN	92·5	96·5	252·5
7. Martin Schmitt	GER	95·0	94·0	250·0
8. Michael Uhrmann	GER	89·0	95·5	245·0

K120 Individual

		FIRST JUMP (M)	SECOND JUMP (M)	TOTAL PTS.
1. Simon Ammann	SWI	132·5	133·0	281·4
2. Adam Malysz	POL	131·0	128·0	269·7
3. Matti Hautamaeki	FIN	127·0	125·5	256·0
4. Sven Hannawald	GER	132·5	131·0	255·3
5. Stefan Horngacher	AUT	125·0	124·0	247·2
6. Andreas Kuttel	SWI	125·0	122·0	245·6
7. Kazuyoshi Funaki	JAP	126·5	121·0	245·5
8. Martin Koch	AUT	126·0	121·5	244·5

Simon Ammann, a farmer's son from the village of Unterwasser in the canton of St Gallen, was a 40kg stripling of sixteen when he competed at the Nagano Olympics, finishing thirty-fifth and thirty-ninth. Four years on, and grown to 1·72m, and still only 52kg, his double triumph on the hills at Park City came as a major surprise. By chance he wore the same start number 53 as did Walter Steiner from neighbouring Wildhaus who was the only previous Swiss winner of an Olympic ski jumping medal in 1972.

Team Jumping

1988 Calgary

			Point Total
1.	FIN	Matti Nykanen 228·8, Ari-Pekka Nikkola 207·9 Jari Puikkonen 193·6, Tuomo Ylipulli 192·3	634.4
2.	YUG	Matjaz Zupan 211·5, Matjaz Debelak 207·5, Primoz Ulaga 207·1, Miran Tepes 192·8	625·5
3.	NOR	Erik Johnsen 218·7, Ole Gunnar Fidjestøl 193·9 Ole Christian Eidhammer 177·2, Jon Inge Kjørum 128·4	596·1
4.	CZE	Pavel Ploc 204·1, Jiri Malek 193·4, Jiri Parma 189·3, Ladislav Dluhos 165·4	586·8
5.	AUT	Gunter Stranner 197·5, Heinz Kuttin 193·3 Ernst Vettori 186	577·6

6.	GER	Thomas Klauser 197·6, Josef Heumann 180·9, Andreas Bauer 175·1, Peter Rohwein 174·3	559·0
7.	SWE	Jan Boklov 180·1. Steffan Tallberg 178·7, Anders Daun 174·2, Inge Tallberg 161·5	539·7
8.	SWI	Gerard Balanche 175·0, Christian Hauswirth 175·0 Fabrice Piazzini 166·2, Christoph Lehmann 156·7	516·1

The 1988 Team event was the first. Eleven nations entered four men with the combined scores of the best three to count. Another stunning performance from Nykanen ensured the Finns the gold medal.

1992 Albertville-Courcheval

			Points Total
1.	FIN	Toni Nieminen 245·0, Ari Pekka Nikkola 225·0, Risto Laakkonen 221·0, Mika Laitinen 216·0	644·4
2.	AUT	Martin Hollwarth 241·0, Heinz Kuttin 227·0, Andreas Felder 224·5, Ernst Vettori 224·0	642·9
3.	CZE	Jiri Parma 234·0, Tomas Goder 227·0, Frantisek Jez 218·0, Jaroslav Sakala 215·0	620·1
4.	JPN	Masahiko Harada 227·0, Jiro Kamiharako 215·1, Kenji Suda 206·5, Noriaki Kasai 203·5	571·0
5.	GER	Dieter Thoma 213·5, Heiko Hunger 212·0, Jens Weissflog 211·0, Christof Duffner 194·5	544·6
6.	SLO	Samo Gostisa 218·5, Franci Petek 212·5, Matjaz Zupan 207·5, Primoz Kipac 195·0	543·3
7.	NOR	Espen Bredesen 223·5, Magne Johansen 206·5, Rune Olijnyk 205·0, Lasse Ottesen 199·0	538·0
8.	SWI	Markus Gahler 214·5, Stefan Zund 214·5, Sylvain Freiholz 209·5, Martin Trunz 198·5	537·9

Early in the first round the jury decided to abandon the competition after some jumpers endangered themselves. Vettori in particular had gone 125·5m. The start point was then lowered and the first round was begun again. In the final round, with only Nieminen and Felder left to jump, the Austrians led the Finns by 30 points, Nieminen then produced a jump of 122m that earned 119·8 points. Felder could only respond with 109·5m, and the Austrians were left 1·5 points adrift.

1994 Lillehammer

			Points Total
1.	GER	Jens Weissflog 277·7, Dieter Thoma 254·1 Christof Duffner 206·5, Hansjorg Jakle 231·8	970·1
2.	JPN	Takanobu Okabe 262·0, Jinya Nishikata 254·4, Noriaki Kasai 248·9, Masahiko Harada 191·6	956·9
3.	AUT	Andreas Goldberger 254·3, Stefan Horngacher 236·6 Heinz Kuttin 216·5, Christian Moser 209·5	918·9
4.	NOR	Espen Bredesen 257·7, Lasse Ottesen 239·8 Øyvind Berg 215·5, Roar Ljokelsoy 185·8	898·5
5.	FIN	Raimo Ylipulli 231·6, Jani Soininen 231·0 Janne Ahonen 214·9, Janne Vaatainen 212·0	889·5
6.	FRA	Nicolas Jean-Prost 224·0, Steve Delaup 203·2 Nicolas Dessum 202·4, Didier Mollard 192·5	822·1
7.	CZE	Zbynek Krompolc 221·9, Jaroslav Sakala 203·9 Ladislav Dluhos 199·8, Jiri Parma 175·1	800·7
8.	ITA	Roberto Cecon 236·2, Ivo Pertile 199·8, Ivan Lunardi 188·5, Andrea Cecon 157·8	782·3

In 1994 the rules were changed. Henceforth the scores of all four team members were added together, instead of those of the best three. After three of the second round jumps, the Japanese had a seemingly unsurmountable lead of 54·9 points. Jens Weissflog, going last for Germany, then produced a sensational leap of 133·5m. Masahiko Harada had jumped 122m in the first round, and needed to go only 105m in reasonable style to ensure victory for Japan. There were questions over his form however, for he had mistimed his second jump in the individual event on the same hill two days before, and had gone only 101m. Again he made the same mistake, and his 97·5m was the shortest made by anyone in the eight top teams.

1998 Nagano

			Points Total
1.	JPN	Takanobu Okabe 259·3, Hiroya Saito 256·2 Masahiko Harada 177·2, Kazuyoshi Funaki 240·3	933·0
2.	GER	Sven Hannawald 258·3, Martin Schmitt 200·1 Hansjorg Jakle 193·6, Dieter Thoma 245·4	897·4
3.	AUT	Reinhard Schwarzengerger 196·5, Martin Hollwarth 241·9, Stefan Horngacher 176·5, Andreas Widholzl 266·6	881·5
4.	NOR	Henning Strensrud 226·2, Lasse Ottesen 205·8 Roar Ljokelsoy 180·9, Kristian Brenden 254·7	870·6

5.	FIN	Ari-Pekka Nikkola 202·9, Mika Laitinen 184·1 Janne Ahonen 213·2, Jani Soininen 233·7	833·9
6.	SWI	Sylvain Freiholz 211·1, Marco Steinauer 175·4 Simon Ammann 117·7, Bruno Reuteler 230·8	735·0
7.	CZE	Jakub Suchacek 149·5, Frantisek Jez 199·1, Michal Dolezal 205·2, Jaroslav Sakala 156·5	710·3
8.	POL	Adam Malysz 190·0, Lukasz Kruczek 165·8 Wojciech Skupien 135·1, Robert Mateja 193·3	684·2

As in 1994, Harada proved to be the weak link in the Japanese team, but his brilliant team mates were able to compensate for his shortcomings and reverse the loss to the Germans at Lillehammer.

2002 Salt Lake City

			Points Total
1.	GER	Sven Hannawald 238·8, Stephan Hocke 222·9 Michael Uhrmann 253·4, Martin Schmitt 259·0	974·1
2.	FIN	Matti Hautamaeki 249·3, Veli-Matti Lindstrom 212·7 Risto Jussilainen 251·4, Janne Ahonen 260·6	974·0
3.	SLO	Damjan Fras 210·4, Primoz Peterka 231·5, Robert Franjek 264·5, Peter Zonta 239·9	946·3
4.	AUT	Stefan Horngacher 221·7, Andreas Widholzl 224·1 Wolfgang Loitzl 239·9, Martin Hollwarth 241·1	926·8
5.	JPN	Masahiko Harada 219·7, Hiroki Yamada 206·8, Hideharu Mirahira 244·5, Kazuyoshi Funaki 255·0	926·0
6.	POL	Robert Mateja 191·4, Tomislaw Tajner 183·3, Tomasz Pochwala 218·4, Adam Malysz 255·0	926·0
7.	SWI	Marco Steinauer 140·4, Sylvain Freiholz 171·7, Andreas Kuttel 236·4, Simon Ammann 269·8	818·3
8.	KOR	Heung Chul Choi 203·4, Yong Jik Choi 191·2, Hyun-Ki Kim 185·8, Chil Gu Kang 221·2	801·6

The Germans won by the smallest possible margin of 0·1 point. The new champion Simon Ammann again produced the longest jumps of the competition, more than doubling his points tally in the same event in 1998, and scoring 33 per cent of the Swiss total. A sub-standard Norwegian team finished in ninth place behind South Korea.

BIBLIOGRAPHY

I am very grateful to Ingrid Christophersen who represents GB on two FIS Committees for a great deal of translation from early Norwegian and German language ski journals. Her father, the late Professor Ragnar Christophersen also gave help and advice. Amongst much else, he was the public commentator to the 120,000 spectators who attended the ski jumping at the 1952 Winter Olympics in Oslo.

Ski records, as compiled by many historians, are notoriously inaccurate, and I am indebted to Rune Flaten, archivist at the museum of the Foreningen til Ski Idretts Fremme in Oslo, for steering me away from myth and error. My thanks also go to Erik Tandberg for his vital work on my behalf in Oslo.

I have also received invaluable assistance from Anne Marie Friedrich, Nordic Officer at the International Ski Federation (FIS) at Oberhofen, and Christian Knauth, Marketing and Communications Director has very kindly given permission to copy photographs from issues of *FIS Bulletin*, and the FIS publication *75 years of Skiing History in Stamps* which appeared in 2000. This extraordinary collection was compiled over his lifetime by the late Jimmy Riddell, a former President of the SCGB, who presented it to the FIS, and saw its publication before he died.

Sources of reference

The Year Books of the following:
  Norges Skiforbund
  Schweizerischer Skiverband
  Osterreicher Skiverband
  Deutscher Skiverband
  The Ski Club of Great Britain

Alpinismus and Wintersports, Illustrierte Allgemeine Alpenzeitung.

The Journals of the American Ski History Society, (Editor: Morten Lund).

FIS Bulletin.

Der Skilauf, Henry Hoek and E.C. Richardson, Munchen 1907, Verlag von Gustav Lammers, Zweite deutsche Auflage.

Der Schi, Henry Hoek, 1922, Bergverlag Rudolf Rother, Munchen.

Wie Lerneich Schilaufen? Henry Hoek, 1925, Bergverlag Rudolf Rother.

Parsenn, Henry Hoek, 1932. Copyright by Gebruder Enoch, Verlag, Hamburg

The Ski Runner, E.C. Richardson, Crichton Somerville and W.R. Rickmers, 1905, Horace Cox.

Out of the Past, Margaret Symonds, 1925, John Murray
Page 223. Robert Louis Stevenson. A letter from her father John Addington Symonds, a fellow resident of Stevenson at Davos, about the writer's 'Treasure Island'.

The Butterflies of Morocco, Algeria and Tunisia, John Tennent, 1996, The Gem Publishing Company, Brightwell cum Sotwell, Wallingford, Oxford, OX10 OQD
Page xix. Colin Wyatt and court appearances, etc.

A History of Skiing, Arnold Lunn, 1927.

Ski Notes and Queries
Ski Survey } Both publications of the Ski Club of GB

Skiløbning, Fritz Huitfeldt, 1908, Jacob Dybwads Forlag, Kristiania
Illustrations of 3 bindings from page 27.

Norsk Ski Tradisjon, Olav Bø, Det Norske, Samlaget 1966.
Portrait photograph of Sondre Norheim which also appears in Halvor Kleppen's book *Telemark Skiing* from page 39; drawing of primitive binding from page 41; an 1862 drawing which appeared in *Illustreret Nyhedsblad*, page 53; drawing of ski jumper with his hat coming off from page 78; a display of 5 ancient bindings from page 87; pencil portrait of Thorleif Haug, from page 106.

Hollmenkollen, Historien og resultatene, Jakob Vaage & Tom Kristensen, De norske Bokklubbene 1971.
Small portrait of Sven Sollid from page 26; Veikko Kankkonen (Finland) at Holmenkollen in 1964 from page 65; Matti Nykanen in the starting gate from page 86; the upper structure of the Holmenkollen with Oslo fjord in background from page 30.

Nansen, Roland Huntford, 1977, Gerald Duckworth.

With Nansen in the North. Lieut Hjalmar Johansen.
English translation published by Ward, Lock & Co Ltd, 1899.

INDEX

Winter Olympics - Albertville '92

90m SKI-JUMP

The GAMBIA D12

RÉPUBLIQUE DE GUINÉE

400 F

XVIèmes JEUX OLYMPIQUES D'HIVER CALGARY 1988

1980 PARAGUAY Gs. 8.

TONI INNAUER - AUSTRIA

LAKE PLACID 1980

20 FMG
ARIARY 4

PAOSITRA 1984

JEUX OLYMPIQUES D'HIVER SARAJEVO-1984

Repoblika Demokratika MALAGASY

SARAJEVO '84

PDR YEMEN

40 FILS POSTAGE

WINTER OLYMPIC GAMES

RÉPUBLIQUE DE DJIBOUTI

POSTES 1988

45 F

Jeux Olympiques d'Hiver
CALGARY 88

LAKE PLACID 1980

60 F

RÉPUBLIQUE DU TCHAD

COMMONWEALTH OF
DOMINICA

Winter Olympics Nagano 1998

Jacob Tullin Thams

$5